BENJAMIN CREME

TRANSMISSION

A Meditation For
The New Age

Fourth Edition

BENJAMIN CREME

Share International Foundation
Amsterdam ❖ London ❖ Los Angeles

*The cover picture is reproduced from a painting by
Benjamin Creme: **OM Overshadowing the Earth**.*

ACKNOWLEDGEMENTS

As always with my books, this book is a product of group work. I am indebted in this case to the contribution of a number of colleagues, particularly in the San Francisco Bay Area. It incorporates material from lectures, seminars, workshops and writings over the past 15 years. This, the fourth, is an expanded and revised edition, and includes a new chapter on alignment as well as various questions and answers which have appeared in *Share International* magazine since the publication of the third edition.

It may be interesting to note that, through the inspiration of my Master, our knowledge of and insight into the underlying purpose of Transmission Meditation has expanded and deepened considerably since the first edition published in March 1983.

BENJAMIN CREME
London, January 1998

EDITOR'S NOTE

The amount of information presented in this book has gradually increased during the past 11 years. The book's first edition, published in March 1983, comprised 80 pages. The present volume, its fourth edition, contains more than twice that number.

The first edition contained information derived solely from Benjamin Creme's public lectures on Transmission Meditation held in the United States in the fall of 1982. As more questions were answered and published subsequently in *Share International* magazine, they were added to the book at each new printing.

As more material became available over the years, new chapters were created. At the Tara Network conferences held in the United States and Holland in 1987, Benjamin Creme presented a talk on "The Role of Transmission Meditation in the Development of the Disciple", and revealed further information — including the underlying purpose of Transmission work. Creme's talk and questions and answers from these conferences were added at the end of the book as Chapter X.

Creme's keynote talk at the Tara Network conferences in 1990 focused on "Discipleship and Practice", and included his (and his Master's) comments on the actual practice of Transmission by disciples during the previous ten years. In-depth discussions followed on how to maintain alignment between the physical brain and the soul, and improve the quality of Transmission work. The material from these discussions is included in the present edition in a new chapter (IX, "Maintaining Alignment"). Although some questions in this new chapter overlap with those in other parts of the book, the information may be expanded upon, or conveyed from a slightly different perspective, and therefore may be useful to the reader.

CONTENTS

VI THE NATURE OF TRANSMISSION 85

PREFACE

MANY PEOPLE HAVE asked me to relate something of the steps which have led me into the work I am now doing. It will not be a complete account: there are unwritten laws of reticence on some aspects of the Master–Disciple relationship; but for whatever interest it may have, and in the hope that it may make more real and believable the fact of the Masters and the fact of the Christ's return at Their head, I set down the following:

As a child of four or five, one of my favorite pastimes was to sit at the window and watch the wind; not the effect of the wind on the trees or leaves, but the wind itself. I would watch the movements of the air and try to guess whether it was a north, south, east or west wind blowing. When I went to school, I learned that the air was invisible, the wind likewise, and forgot my ability to see what of course was some level of the etheric planes of matter.

Above the dense physical — solid, liquid, and gaseous — are four planes of still finer matter which constitute the etheric envelope of this planet, and of which the dense physical planes are a precipitation. It was not until some twenty years later, through the building and use of Wilhelm Reich's orgone accumulator, that I again became aware of this ocean of energy of which we ourselves are a part, and proved to myself conclusively the existence of the etheric planes.

I became consciously aware of and extremely sensitive to energy currents; so much so that eventually I could tell when an atomic bomb had been exploded in the Pacific or anywhere else in the world. Across these thousands of miles, I registered the shift in the etheric currents caused by the explosions. Inevitably, a day or two later would come the report that America, Russia, or Britain had tested a 'device' of such and such a size. . . .

I read, among many others, the Theosophical works of H. P. Blavatsky and Leadbeater; Gurdjieff, Ouspensky and Nicoll;

Paul Brunton; Patanjali; the Alice Bailey and Agni Yoga teachings; Swamis Vivekananda, Sivananda, Yogananda; Sri Ramana Maharshi, whose Path of Self-Knowledge I sought to follow. Through his meditation on "Who am I?" (and, I know now, through the Grace of my Master), I found myself precipitated into a sense of identity with the whole phenomenal world: the earth, the sky, the houses and people, the trees and birds and clouds, I saw to be myself. I disappeared as a separate being, yet retained full consciousness, a consciousness expanded to include everything. I saw that this was the true Reality, that one's normal waking consciousness simply covers this, keeps it hidden, through wrong identification with oneself as this body. I also saw this phenomenal world as a kind of ritual, a ritualized shadow-play, acting out a dream or desire of That which alone existed, alone was Real, which was also myself. . . .

In late 1958, I was told by a fellow disciple who had the 'connection' that I was receiving "messages". This surprised me and I had no sense that it was true. I was told that the messages "bounced off" me, but if I did such and such, in time I would receive correctly.

I must have done the right thing, because one night, early in January 1959, so clearly there was no mistaking, I heard inwardly the instruction: Go to so and so (a place in London) on such and such a date and time, some three weeks ahead. On the night, there were people waiting there to meet me.

That was the start of a flow of messages which came in gathering momentum. Some, apparently, I missed (I was told later when I missed one) and I became so afraid of missing them that I gave them to myself. I sent myself on several rendezvous, where nothing happened and no one came, but gradually I settled down; I did not miss them and I stopped making them up.

I was told to get a tape-recorder and received many long dictations of various kinds. Some contained advice, guidance, or spiritual instruction. I was not told the identity of the Master (or Masters) Who spoke thus, telepathically, to me, and I think I was too shy to ask, although I was told I could ask questions. It was not until years later that I learned His name and also that I would have been told had I asked long ago.

One night, early in 1959, during such a transmission, I was told to turn off the tape-recorder. There followed a discourse on His Reappearance by Maitreya, the Christ, Head of our Planetary Hierarchy. He said also that I would have a part in the Plan. At that time I believed that the World Teacher would come from one of the higher planets, probably from Venus, and this information from Maitreya caused a complete upset to my thinking. In a transmission soon after this event, my Master, referring to this new-found knowledge, added: **"The time is coming when you will be expected to act upon it."** And in another: **"Affirm His coming!"**

I cannot claim that I took these exhortations to heart and that that is why I am engaged in this work of preparation for the Christ. On instruction, I put these tapes away for seventeen years and I am afraid I needed a rather strong push from the Master to launch me into this work.

Towards the end of 1972, when I was rather in the doldrums and least expecting it, that Wise and Wily One Whom I have the privilege to call Master, pounced. He took me in hand, and subjected me to the most intensive period of de-glamorization, disillusioning, training, and preparation. For months we worked together, twenty hours a day, deepening and strengthening the telepathic link until it was two-way with equal ease, requiring the minimum of His attention and energy. He forged in this period an instrument through whom He could work, and which would be responsive to His slightest impression (of course, with my complete co-operation and without the slightest infringement of my free will). Everything I see and hear, He sees and hears. When He wishes, a look from me can be a look from Him; my touch, His. So, with the minimum expenditure of energy He has a window on the world, an outpost of His consciousness; He can heal and teach. He Himself remains, in a fully physical body, thousands of miles away. I am not suggesting that I am His only "window on the world". I do not know how rare this is, but I am

3

sure that it is not unique. It constitutes a definite stage in the Master–Disciple relationship. He has asked me not to reveal His identity for the time being, not even to the members of the group with which I work, and through which He works. I know of two reasons (there may be others) for His request, and respect them, but I may say that He is one of the Senior Members of the Hierarchy, a Master of the Wisdom, Whose name is well known to esotericists in the West. His inspiration has heightened tremendously the conceptual power and intensity of my paintings. . . .

In March 1974, He gave me a list of 14 names of people to invite to a talk at my home on "meditation and allied subjects". They all came.

I talked about the Hierarchy of Masters, about meditation, and its role in bringing about soul contact. Under instruction, I presented them with the following offer: I invited them to take part in a group work in which their occult meditation would proceed under the guidance of a Master of the Wisdom, in exchange for which they would act as transmitters of the Hierarchical energies, thus forming a bridging group between Hierarchy and the disciples in the field.

The Master arranged a short Transmission to show them what was involved. Twelve of the 14 agreed, two feeling that they were not ready for this kind of work.

The group was formed in March 1974 to channel the spiritual potencies. We met twice weekly, at first, for about one-and-a-half to two hours. The question of a name for the group came up, but the Master's instruction was, and still is, that no name should be used; no organization built; no officers appointed; no fences erected around ourselves and our ideas; the maximum openness maintained.

At the same time, the Master gave me the blueprint for building the transmitter/transformer instrument which we use in this work, and which I also use in healing. It is a tetrahedron in form and is based on the principle that certain shapes have inherent energetic properties.

A great study is going on today into the nature and energetic properties of the pyramid. The Great Pyramid at Giza is really an Atlantean instrument, based on the power of shape. The aim of Atlantean man was to perfect the astral-emotional vehicle, or body. Just by being the shape it is, the pyramid, when aligned with the north and south poles, draws energy from the etheric and astral planes. This was transmitted for the benefit of the population of the great city which lies buried beneath the sands around the Pyramid and the Sphinx.

The aim of our present, fifth, root race, the Aryan, is to perfect the mental vehicle. When aligned north and south, the Tetrahedron automatically draws to itself and transmits energy from the mental planes. This principle is behind our use of the instrument. The instrumentation — quartz crystal, magnets, gold and silver discs, and wires — focuses and potentizes all the energies channelled through us by Hierarchy; the shape itself transforming them downwards on to the lower mental planes where they can be more readily absorbed by many people. Without this transforming work, which the instrument carries further, the Hierarchical energies, streaming as they do in the main from the Buddhic level (the level of the Spiritual Intuition), would "bounce off" the masses of people, and their effect would be limited. This is behind the need of Hierarchy for transmission groups, using some form of meditation or prayer.

Under the Master's instruction, I built also a Spiritual Energy Battery which can be attached to the transmitter. So far we have used it only once, to demonstrate, I suppose, the principle.

The group's personnel has changed many times, only four of the original group remaining. Its numbers have grown and fallen, but always seem to stabilize at around 12 fully active members, with many less active or regular participants, and with a great many offshoot groups, both here and abroad. Nowadays, we meet regularly three times weekly to transmit the energies from Hierarchy for anything from four to seven or eight hours on end. Only the most dedicated and committed people, of course, can maintain that intensity of rhythm, so numbers are, necessarily, kept low. In addition, we hold a regular weekly public meeting at the Friends Meeting House, Euston Road, London, in which the audience is invited to share in the transmission of the energies which are sent.

In June 1974 began a series of overshadowings and transmitted messages by Maitreya, inspiring us, and keeping us informed of the progress of His externalization. We were privileged also to become aware of the gradual creation and perfection of His body of manifestation — the mayavirupa. In the period from March 1976 to September 1977, these communications from Maitreya became very frequent indeed.

During the first year of the group's life, we held an open meeting at each full moon where interested friends of the members could join in the transmission. At these full-moon meetings, I would give a short talk, usually about the Reappearance of the Christ and the Hierarchy of Masters, or, on occasion, on the significance, from an esoteric astrological point of view, of the particular full-moon energies.

Towards the end of 1974, the Master said, several times: "You know, you must take all this to the public. It is of little use giving this information to only the 20 or so people who are here." The pantomime began: I would remonstrate, plead not to have to "go public". He would assure me that He was only joking: "I have other plans for you," He would say, and I would relax again. But in January 1975 He finally said: "I mean it. Give this information (He had dictated a mass of information on how the Plan would work out) to the groups, of all backgrounds and teachings. Tell them what you know. The hope is that from the more focused minds of the groups will go out a telepathic interplay with the general public, so that when you go to them, they will be somewhat prepared."

I didn't like it. I didn't like it at all. I liked what I was doing. I liked working quietly, esoterically, knowing I was doing something useful, but neither too strenuous nor making too great psychological demands on me. I did nothing about the groups until several firm pushes from the Master at last got me moving. In March or April, I wrote hopefully to 40 or so groups working along spiritual lines, offering my services as a speaker on: "The Reappearance of the Christ and the Masters of the Wisdom". The response, not surprisingly, for I was quite unknown, was not altogether overwhelming. I had, I think, about six or seven replies. Three of these groups were interested to know more — all newish groups run by young people — Centre House, Gentle Ghost and the Franklin School, and I gave a talk at each, the first at Centre House, on 30 May 1975.

I was very nervous. Although I knew my material, I did not have it in any sort of order. The Master, in His kindness, dictated for me a list of headings which I could glance at, and, in fact, so overshadowed me throughout the talk that He practically gave it. Just before the end, I was suddenly overshadowed by Maitreya Himself, my heart melted, and I had the greatest difficulty in keeping my voice steady. The following words were put into my mind:

"When the Christ returns, He will not at first reveal His Presence, nor will the Masters Who precede Him; but gradually, steps will be taken which will reveal to men that there lives among them now a man of outstanding, extraordinary, potency, capacity for love and service, and with a breadth of view, far beyond the ordinary. Men and women, all over the world, will find themselves drawn into the awareness of the point in the modern world wherein this man will live; and from that centre of force will flow the True Spirit of the Christ, which will gradually reveal to men that He is with us. Those who can respond to His Presence and His Teaching will find themselves somewhat reflecting this love, this potency, this breadth of vision, and will go into the world and spread abroad the fact that the Christ is in the world, and that men should look to that country from which a certain Teaching is emanating. This will take place in a very, relatively, short period of time, and will lead to conclusive evidence that the Christ is in our midst.

7

"From that time onwards, the changes which will take place in the world will proceed with a speed unprecedented in the whole history of the planet. The next 25 years will show such changes, changes so radical, so fundamental, that the world will be entirely changed for the better."

No one was more surprised than I was to hear this statement. Not until I heard it back on tape was I sure, even, that it made sense.

On 7 July 1977, Maitreya Himself informed us that His body of manifestation was totally complete, that He had "donned" it, and that His Body of Light (His Ascended Body) was now at rest in His mountain Centre in the Himalayas. On 8 July, we were told, the Descent had begun. On Tuesday, 19 July, my Master told me that Maitreya had now arrived in His "point of focus", a well-known modern country. I had a lecture meeting that night at Friends House, but was told to keep the information to myself as yet. During our Friday Transmission session, the Master told me that Maitreya had been resting, acclimatizing Himself, for three days, and that on that day, 22 July. His Mission had begun. This information I was allowed to share with the group.

About midnight, the transmission ended and we congregated as usual for tea before dispersing. My wife turned on the television, where the late-night film featured some family drama with Bette Davis in the leading role. Some of the group watched, but, understandably, my thoughts were elsewhere. I made some sarcastic remarks about the film and its actors (usually I admire Bette Davis as an actress very much). When I could bear it no longer, I said I had some rather more important news to tell them — that the Christ was now in the everyday world in full, physical Presence, and beginning His Mission.

Many, many times since, to scores of audiences, I have made this announcement, but never again with the sense of having, even in a small way, shared in a great planetary event. The tears of joy on the faces of the group around the table showed that they, too, felt the same.

At the beginning of September 1977, I was asked if I would take the messages from Maitreya publicly. On 6 September 1977, the first public message was given, at Friends' House, Euston Road, "experimentally", to find out, I suppose, how I stood up to the demonstration of this kind of overshadowing and telepathy in public — a very different thing from the privacy of one's own group. These have continued until now. At the moment of going to press we have received 85 messages. These are conveyed by me to the audience; no trance or mediumship is involved, and the voice is mine, very obviously strengthened in power and altered in pitch by the overshadowing energy of Maitreya. They are transmitted simultaneously on all the astral and mental planes, while I supply the basic etheric-physical vibration for this to take place. From these subtle levels, the messages impress the minds and hearts of countless people, who are gradually made aware of the thoughts and the Presence of the Christ. He releases in this way fragments of His Teaching, to prepare the climate of hope and expectancy which will ensure His being accepted and followed, quickly and gladly.

It is an enormous, and embarrassing, claim to have to make — that the Christ is giving messages through oneself. But if people can rid their minds of the idea of the Christ as some sort of spirit, sitting in "heaven" at God's right hand; if they can begin to see Him as indeed He is, as a real and living man (albeit a Divine man) who has never left the world; who descended, not from "heaven", but from His ancient retreat in the Himalayas, to complete the task He began in Palestine; as a great Master; an Adept and Yogi; as the chief actor in a Gospel Story which is essentially true, but much simpler than hitherto presented; if people can accept that possibility, then the claim to receive telepathic communications from such a closer and more knowable Being is also, perhaps, more acceptable. In any case, I leave it to a study of the quality of the Messages themselves to convince or otherwise. For many people, the energies, which flow during the overshadowing, convince. Many who come to these meetings are clairvoyant in various degrees, and their visions of the overshadowing as it takes place is for them the most convincing evidence of all.

Perhaps the above will help explain why I speak of the Masters and the Christ and Their reappearance with conviction. For me, Their existence is a fact, known through my direct experience and contact. It is in the hope of awakening others to the reality of that fact, and to the further momentous fact of Their return now to the everyday world to lead us into the Aquarian Age, that this is written.

BENJAMIN CREME
London 1979

(The above are excerpts taken from the Preface to *The Reappearance of the Christ and the Masters of Wisdom* by Benjamin Creme.)

CHAPTER I

INTRODUCTION:
WHAT IS TRANSMISSION MEDITATION?

TRANSMISSION MEDITATION is a form of meditation which is also a transmission of energy. We would not be human beings if we did not knowingly or unknowingly act as transmitters of energy. If the human kingdom were for some reason or other removed from this planet, all the lower kingdoms — animal, vegetable and even mineral — would eventually die. They would no longer receive their quota of energy from the sun at a potency which they could absorb. This is because the human kingdom (as do all kingdoms) transmits energy, albeit in a unique fashion. Whether we know it or not (and in the future we shall know it and act consciously as such), we are transmitters, a clearinghouse for energies received from the kingdoms above us. These energies are transformed by passing through us to the lower kingdoms.

Each kingdom evolves as a result of the stimulus from the kingdom immediately above it. The physical form comes from below and the spiritual stimulus towards evolution from above.

The vegetable kingdom grew out of the mineral kingdom, the first kingdom to be laid down and the most inert. Out of the vegetable kingdom has grown the animal kingdom; from the animal, the human kingdom. (We owe our physical bodies to the animal kingdom.) Out of the human kingdom, whether humanity knows it or not, has grown and is growing the Spiritual Kingdom, the Kingdom of Souls, or, in Christian terminology, the Kingdom of God.

The Kingdom of God, the Spiritual Kingdom, is not some blessed state which has to come down from heaven when humanity is good enough, developed enough, to receive it. It is something which, unknown to most of us, has always existed behind the scenes of our life. It is made up of the Masters and Initiates of the Wisdom, of that group of men and women who have gone ahead of us, evolved before us, and, in the case of the Masters, have come to the end of the evolutionary experience on this planet.

The Masters serve the plan of evolution of the human and subhuman kingdoms. They are the custodians of all the energies entering the planet. Powerful cosmic energies impinge upon this planet from everywhere in space. We know nothing about them and can do nothing with them since we do not have that science, but the Masters work with these energies, scientifically balancing them and sending them into the world to help humanity evolve. The Masters are the key figures in this process, working from behind the scenes through men and women, the initiates, the disciples, and aspirants in the world.

Humanity evolves through the correct absorption of the spiritual energies from the Kingdom of Souls. All change, on both an individual and a world-wide scale, is the result of our response to great spiritual forces. We do not see these energies for the most part, but nevertheless they are there. They work through us, and as we respond — by changing and creating new structures, making personal, communal, international decisions — we are responding to these energies.

The energies are of very many different kinds and qualities, and therefore have different names. One is called Will; another is Love. We think of 'love' as the kind of emotion that people feel between each other. Of course emotion has something to do with Love but at a lower level of the great cosmic energy. Love, which the Masters send into the world in its pure form, is the cohesive, magnetic force binding the atoms of matter and the units of humanity together.

The evolutionary aim is that we shall be bound together by the energy of Love and demonstrate it in our lives. Unfortunately, humanity as a whole does not do this as yet, but in the coming Age of Aquarius we shall manifest the quality of

Love just as powerfully and clearly and correctly as today we demonstrate the energy which we call Knowledge. Our science and technology are the direct result of our ability today to manifest the energy of Knowledge. Two thousand years ago we could not do so.

The Christ came in Palestine to show us Love, to show us that the nature of divinity is Love, and He demonstrated perfect Love in a human being for the first time. In 2,000 years we still have not manifested that quality which He released into the world. Of course, many men and women have individually realized within themselves the quality of Love and have become disciples, initiates, and in some cases Masters of the Wisdom. Through the demonstration of the Love of God, They have reached the relative perfection which the Masters know, a perfection that one day will be our own destiny to manifest.

The promise of this coming Age of Aquarius is that, for the first time in recorded human history, humanity will become One and will demonstrate the Love of which unity is the expression. It will reflect on the physical plane the inner oneness of man — the fact that as souls we are One. There is no such thing as a separate soul. We are individualized parts of one great Oversoul which is perfect, and which is a reflection of what we call God, of that Reality in which we "live and move and have our being" — the Logos of the planet.

The true purpose of the soul in incarnation is to carry out the Will and the Plan of the Logos of the planet. It is a sacrifice for the soul, a perfected spiritual being in its own right — our true Higher Self — to express itself on the dense physical plane through the apparatus of the physical, emotional, and mental bodies, integrated by this personality whom we take to be ourselves. Every single one of us is divine. However, it is extremely difficult to manifest that divinity in its perfection, exactly as it is, at this level, because that divinity has immersed itself in matter. When the soul incarnates, it takes a vehicle composed of material energy which inhibits the reflection of the divine Purpose (Will, Love, Intelligence) of the soul, because the energy of matter is inert and unrefined. The purpose of coming into incarnation again and again, thousands upon thousands of times through the evolutionary journey, is gradually to spiritualize the matter of the planet. This is what we are really engaged in doing, and initially we do it through spiritualizing the matter of our own bodies.

All the Masters are living in perfected bodies (resurrected bodies, in the Biblical sense of resurrection) which are literally light, although they are solid and physical like yours and mine. Gradually, through the incarnational process, the soul brings to each body more and more sub-atomic matter which is literally light. And as this occurs, we also demonstrate, gradually, the nature of the soul. We become ensouled.

Towards the end phase of our evolutionary journey our soul brings us into meditation. In the first life in which this occurs, it may be fleeting, but some contact with meditation is made. In the next life much more is made, until after several lifetimes, meditation becomes a natural activity of the individual in incarnation. This eventually makes the journey inward to the soul automatic.

The purpose of our evolutionary existence, then, is to manifest the soul's qualities on the physical plane, and so to spiritualize matter. Meditation provides a more-or-less scientific means, depending on the meditation, of contacting the soul and gradually becoming at-one with the soul, so that it can manifest clearly and potently on the physical plane. When we see such individuals, we perceive them as radiating meaning and purpose — for example, exceptionally creative artists, scientists, politicians, or educators. Such persons are quite obviously governed by a force altogether different from the norm. It is the energy of the soul which is pouring through them, making them the creative beings who enrich our culture and civilization.

Transmission Meditation is the simplest method I know to accomplish this soul contact. Many meditations require that the individual master a powerful concentrated mental activity, which is more than most people can do. What people call meditation is often not meditation but simply concentration or even just reverie. There are five stages of meditation, each one leading gradually into the next: concentration, meditation, contemplation, illumination, and inspiration. Transmission Meditation can enhance all of these.

Since the declaration by the Christ in 1945 that He would reappear at the earliest possible moment, there is as never before an enormous potency of energy at the disposal of the Masters. When He made that decision, He became the channel for colossal cosmic and extra-systemic spiritual forces. These need to be 'stepped down', or they simply bounce off the bulk of humanity. By the work of Transmission Meditation groups, however, these forces become transformed and readily available and accessible.

In a Transmission group, you simply let yourself be an instrument, while the energy is put through your chakras by the Masters. You act as a positive, poised, mental channel through which the energy is sent in a highly scientific manner. It is directed by Them, by Their thought, to where it is most useful and most needed. They are always looking for those who can consciously act as transmitters of Their energy in this way.

To form a Transmission Meditation group, all you need is the intention and desire to serve, and two other people who agree to transmit with you. Of course, the more people the better, but three in itself is a group. The meditation used is simple, but it is the most dynamic I know. It requires no extraordinary expertise. It is a simple aligning meditation — the alignment of the physical brain and the soul by the act of holding the attention at the ajna centre between the eyebrows.

You might say: "That's all very well to say, 'Sit down and meditate,' but how do we get hold of these energies which we've got to transmit?" Humanity has been given an extraordinarily potent tool whereby the energy of the Masters can be invoked at will. It is called the Great Invocation. The Christ Himself used it for the first time in June 1945, when He announced to His Brothers, the Masters of the Wisdom, that He was ready to return to the world at the earliest possible moment, as soon as humanity took the first steps towards sharing and co-operation for the general good. It was translated by the Masters and released to the world by the Tibetan Master Djwhal Khul through His amanuensis Alice A. Bailey.

The Great Invocation is a very potent prayer. By its use, any group of transmitters can invoke the energies of the Christ and the Masters, and, acting as instruments, allow these energies to pass through their chakras in a simple, pleasant, and scientific manner.

The important thing is regularity. What is required is for the group to meet regularly, at least once a week, always at the same time. In this way the Masters can depend on a group of individuals being physically present at that time. By the use of the Great Invocation, the group aligns itself with the Hierarchy, and the Masters transmit the energies through the group to the world. This process of Transmission will go on into the New Age and beyond, for as long as humanity exists.

The Masters transmit energy all the time. They are the custodians of the destiny of this planet. You are safe in the hands of the Masters of the Wisdom.

A huge network of light is being created by the Christ on the soul plane and it is growing all the time. Each Transmission group is linked into this network and a tremendous spiritual power radiates along it throughout the world.

YOGA OF THE NEW AGE

Transmission Meditation is really a combination of two yogas: Karma Yoga — the yoga of service, and Laya Yoga — the yoga of the chakras, the energies. This is the true yoga of the coming age. By taking part in Transmission Meditation, your evolution is propelled forward at an extraordinary rate, because of the potency of the spiritual energies sent through the chakras. The energies galvanize and activate the chakras as they pass through them. The Masters register the point in evolution of any individual by looking at the state of the chakras.

To take part in Transmission Meditation, you only have to hold your attention at the ajna centre. In practice you will find that the attention will not stay there. It will keep dropping to its usual level somewhere around the solar plexus. As soon as the attention drops and you become aware of that, you have to bring it back to the ajna centre. This is done by thinking, inwardly, the mantram OM. As soon as you think OM, you find that your attention automatically comes back to the ajna centre. While your attention is held at the ajna centre, a connection, or alignment is formed between the physical brain and the soul. The energies do not come from your soul. They come from the Masters, from the Kingdom of Souls. But they proceed from the soul level. While the alignment between the physical brain and the soul is kept, you are in the Transmission. As soon as your attention drops from the ajna centre, you are no longer taking part. As you think OM, the attention rises again, you are aligned. The process is one of being aligned, for a moment not aligned, and then, once again, aligned, back and forth.

The easiest way to do Transmission Meditation is to join an already-existing group. If there is no group in your area within a reasonable distance, you can form your own group by joining with two other people. More people are more useful, but a basic group of three is a practical working group. If you have one group of three people, you have one triangle. The energy is triangulated, which potentizes it. If you have one more person, you have four triangles, which potentizes it more. If you have one more person, five, you have ten triangles — and so on, in arithmetical progression. The more people, the more triangles, the more powerful is the group. It is so powerful that in one year of correct, sustained Transmission Meditation you can make the same kind of advance as in 10, 15, or even 20 years of ordinary meditation. But the true, fundamental purpose of Transmission Meditation is service to the world. The world needs these energies from the Masters at the level that they can be absorbed and used. These are the energies that transform life on the planet.

DEFINITION OF TERMS

You refer to the New Age or the coming Age of Aquarius. What do you really mean by this?

Almost everyone has heard about the dawn of a new age but relatively few, it would appear, understand what is meant by the phrase, or how it comes about. In strictly scientific terms it is the result of the precession of the equinoxes. In laymen's terminology, it is the result of the movement of our solar system round the heavens in relation to the constellations of the zodiac. The complete cycle lasts approximately 26,000 years, and every 2,150 years, more or less, our sun comes into alignment with each constellation in turn. When this occurs, our system and, of course, our planet receive a great inflow of energies from that constellation. For the last 2,500 years, our solar system has been in that special relationship to the constellation, Pisces. We have been in the age of Pisces. The Christ inaugurated that age 2,000 years ago. It is for this reason that the fish, the symbol for Pisces, was adopted by the early Christian groups.

We have come to the end of that age, our sun has moved into alignment with Aquarius, and the new, altogether different, energies of Aquarius are daily growing in potency and impact on our lives. The trouble-torn time in which we live is the result of the confrontation, on all levels and in every department of life, between the energies, now receding, of Pisces, and the incoming forces of Aquarius.

What do you mean by "energy"?

There is an ancient esoteric axiom that there is nothing in the whole manifested universe except energy in some relationship, at some vibrational frequency. Wherever we look, whatever we can conceive, is really energy more or less concretized, vibrating at a particular frequency. All of these points of energy are in relationship. There is a reciprocal interplay between all aspects of the universe. We are literally a whole, a unity. Modern physicists, exploring the nature of the atom, have come to exactly the same conclusion about the nature of reality as that arrived at by the ancient Masters. There is nothing in all reality but energy. All that we think of as God can be known in terms of energy. The development of man towards God is the development of consciousness, the creation of a sensitive apparatus or instrument responsive to higher and higher levels of the sum total of energies, and laws governing these energies, which we call God. This is how we become divine: we gradually tune into, become aware of, and radiate the energy which is God.

What is a chakra?

A chakra is a vortex or centre of force. For example, our solar system is a centre of force through which energy from the galaxy can be transmitted. Our planet is a chakra in the body of that great cosmic being who ensouls this solar system, who to us is God.

Chakras are formed by the interweaving of energies on the etheric planes of matter. We recognize three states of matter — solid, liquid, and gaseous physical. But esotericists recognize and use four further states of matter finer than gas — the four etheric planes. We live in an ocean of etheric energies. The etheric envelope of the world is concentrated in the etheric body of the human being. All of us have a counterpart etheric body which substands the dense physical body and is an exact replica of it. The constant movement of the ocean of etheric energy gradually creates vortices where the energies criss-cross most often. Each vortex is a chakra, an opening into and out of the body, and all the energies impinging on the etheric physical body flow through these force centres.

19

There are seven chakras up the spine, located at the base of the spine, the sacrum, the solar plexus, the heart, the throat, between the eyebrows and at the top of the head. These are the seven major centres. There are 42 minor centres and many subsidiary centres — for example, the cheeks, the earlobes, the palms of the hands. Through these centres energies flow most potently. In Transmission Meditation, the activity of these centres is heightened and stimulated.

What is the relationship between Spirit, soul, and the physical person?

The soul is the reflection of the Spirit (or Monad, in Theosophical terminology). The Spirit is identical with the Logos. It is the Spark of God, our true nature. We are constituted on three levels: (1) the Monad or Spirit, the highest; this is reflected lower on the soul level as (2) the human ego or soul; the soul reflects itself on the physical plane as (3) the human personality. When we look in the mirror, we think we are seeing ourselves, but we are seeing only a tiny tip of the iceberg. Above the personality is the soul with all its areas of experience and knowledge. Above the soul, reflected through it, is the Monad, or Spirit, the Spark of God, which is the source and guarantee of the divinity of man. We are divine because we are made literally in the image of the Logos who ensouls this planet.

The purpose of the soul is a sacrificial one. The soul incarnates at the human level through its personality vehicles — mental, astral, and physical — in sacrifice for the plan of the Logos. The plan and purpose of the Logos is to spiritualize the aspect of itself which we call matter.

Spirit and matter are two poles of one reality. Spirit has involved itself in matter, its polar opposite. Man is the midway point between spirit and matter. Where Father/Spirit and Mother/Matter meet, man, humanity, is born. The Monad descends and reflects itself as the soul; the soul descends and reflects itself as the physical plane personality — the man or woman that we see. At a certain point, the journey back again begins. In the process of evolving back to the Spirit, we spiritualize the matter of our successive bodies, from the first incarnational experience to the last, leading to the resurrection experience which makes us the perfected Master. In that way we spiritualize the planet. Humanity is really engaged in the task of salvation, of spiritualizing the material substance of this planet. The transmission of energy is one of the services whereby that procedure can go forward.

Chapter II

The Great Invocation

From the point of Light within the Mind of God
Let light stream forth into the minds of men.
Let Light descend on Earth.

From the point of Love within the Heart of God
Let love stream forth into the hearts of men.
May Christ return to Earth.

From the centre where the Will of God is known
Let purpose guide the little wills of men —
The Purpose which the Masters know and serve.

From the centre which we call the race of men
Let the Plan of Love and Light work out.
And may it seal the door where evil dwells.

Let Light and Love and Power
Restore the Plan on Earth.

THIS GREAT INVOCATION, used by the Christ for the first time in June 1945, was released by Him to humanity to enable man himself to invoke the energies which would change our world, and make possible the return of the Christ and Hierarchy. This is not the form of it used by the Christ. He uses an ancient formula, seven mystic phrases long, in an ancient sacerdotal tongue. It has been translated (by Hierarchy) into terms which we can use and understand and, translated into many languages, is used today in almost every country in the world.

Potent as it is, it can be made even more so if used in triangular formation. If you wish to work in this way, arrange with two friends to use the Invocation, aloud, daily. You need not be in the same town, or country, or say it at the same time of day. Simply say it when convenient for each one, and, linking up mentally with the two other members, visualize a triangle of white light circulating above your heads and see it linked to a network of such triangles, covering the world.

Another very potent way, which can be used in conjunction with the triangle, is the following:

When you say the first line: "From the point of Light . . .", visualize (or think of, if you cannot visualize) the Buddha, the Embodiment of Light or Wisdom on the planet. Visualize Him sitting in the lotus position, saffron robe over one shoulder, hand raised in blessing, and see emanating from the heart centre, the ajna centre (between the eyebrows), and the upraised hand of the Buddha, a brilliant golden light. See this light enter the minds of men everywhere.

When you say the line: "Let Light descend on Earth", visualize the physical sun, and see emanating from it beams of white light. See this light enter and saturate the earth.

When you say: "From the point of Love . . .", visualize the Christ (the Embodiment of Love) however you see Him. A good way is to see Him standing at the head of an inverted Y-shaped table: **ʎ**, with each arm of the **ʎ** of the same length. (That table exists in the world, and the Christ presides at it.) See Him standing, arms raised in blessing, and see emanating from the heart centre and the upraised hands of the Christ, a brilliant rose-coloured light (not red). Visualize this rose light entering the hearts of men everywhere.

When you say the line: "May Christ return to Earth", remember that this refers to the Hierarchy as a whole and not only to the Christ. He is the heart centre of the Hierarchy, and although He is now among us, the remainder of the Hierarchy (that part of it which will externalize slowly over the years) still

24

must be invoked, so the magnetic conduit for Their descent must be maintained.

When you say: "From the centre where the Will of God is known", (which is Shamballa) visualize a great sphere of white light. (You can place it, mentally, in the Gobi desert, where it is, on the two highest of the four etheric planes. One day, when mankind develops etheric vision, which it will do in this coming age, this centre will be seen and known, as many other etheric centres will be seen and known.) Visualize beams of light streaming from this brilliant sphere, entering the world, galvanizing mankind into spiritual action.

Do this with focused thought and intention, your attention fixed on the ajna centre between the eyebrows. In this way you form a telepathic conduit between yourselves and Hierarchy and through that conduit the energies thus invoked can flow. There is nothing better you can do for the world or yourselves than to channel these great spiritual potencies.

Where did the visualization for the Great Invocation come from, and why is there no visualization for the fourth stanza?

The visualization was given to me by my Master for the use of Transmission groups and anyone else who wishes to use it. No visualization was given for the fourth stanza, which relates not to a source of energy but to its working out in the world.

I have some difficulty with the Great Invocation. My difficulty stems from the statements in it: "From the point of Light within the Mind of God, let light stream forth into the minds of men." That puts God out there to me. I think God is in every one of us. It's the energy you talked about. So I'm not comfortable using it.

God is both out there and within. The Christ taught that God is within. Nevertheless, the general view of God in the western world is to see God as out there, transcendent, above and beyond its creation, having no real contact with that creation, to be worshipped and prayed to from afar. The eastern approach is

25

quite different. It is to the God within. The eastern religions have taught that God is everywhere, that there is nowhere where God is not. God is in all creation — men, animals, trees, everything. There is nothing in the manifested world which is not God. All beings and the space between all beings are God, "closer than hand or foot, closer even than the breath" — God immanent.

Both approaches are right. God is both transcendent and immanent. In a new world religion, the Christ will bring together these two concepts of God. He will synthesize them and show that God is transcendent, above and beyond man and all creation, while at the same time intrinsic, immanent in all creation. Both concepts are true, and both can be held simultaneously even if they seem to be contradictory. That will be the basic approach to God of the New World Religion. Christ comes as the World Avatar uniting East and West precisely through that double concept of God.

The Great Invocation does not really refer specifically to God. It says: "From the point of Light within the Mind of God." The Light within the Mind of God is an energy embodied in this world by a great Being — the Buddha. You are invoking the energy from Him. God always works through agents — those who have manifested so much of the immanence of God in their own being that they can actually embody certain great energies. The Buddha embodies the Light or Wisdom of God. He is still on this planet in a great centre called Shamballa. He is the point of Light within the Mind of God, the embodiment of the light, or wisdom principle on this planet.

So you are not making God transcendent at all. You are seeing God in terms of His Representatives. The Buddha and the Christ are Representatives of God, embodiments of two aspects of divine energy: Wisdom and Love.

The Love of God is a great energy originating in the sun. It holds the particles of matter in the universe together and holds the units of humanity together. Humanity may not yet realize that the cement, the cohesive force which ties us together, is

Love. That is why Love "makes the world go round", as we say. Without it, we would all literally fall apart. The world is falling apart now because there is not enough love in the world.

Actually, there is an abundance of love, but we do not express it. We do not manifest the energy of love. It is pouring into this world daily, hourly, in tremendous potency from the One who embodies it, the Christ. But where you have non-utilization and non-manifestation of that energy, you have chaos.

Love is an active force. It becomes love only when it is in action. It is no good saying: "I love you. I love everyone," and then actually giving nothing, doing nothing, to redress the awful imbalances in the world situation. Millions are starving in a world of plenty. Where is the love? We do not have the right to say "I love" while we do nothing to change the poverty, starvation and human degradation which exist in the world.

When you say: "From the centre where the Will of God is known", you are invoking the energy from Shamballa. Shamballa is the centre where God reflects Himself on this planet. When you use that line in the Great Invocation, you are actually invoking the energy of Will, which embodies the Purpose of God. Flowing through us, it becomes manifested and usable in the world.

You are seeing God in real terms, manifesting potently in the Buddha, in the Christ, and most potently of all in Shamballa. These are realities.

When we say: "May Christ return to Earth", do we mean the Christ consciousness now that the Christ and 12 Masters are already here?

No. The Christ consciousness is an energy — the energy of evolution itself — embodied by the Christ for this period of human crisis. Since His decision to reappear, announced in June 1945, this energy has flowed into the world in enormously renewed potency. "May Christ return to Earth" should now be said in relation to the Spiritual Hierarchy as a whole. Only 12 Masters (besides Maitreya) are in the world, but there are 63 Masters connected with the human evolution. Of these, some two-thirds will eventually take Their places among us, slowly, over about 20 years. The Invocation forms a telepathic conduit which draws Them, under law, into the world. [*Editor's note*: 14 Masters as of 1997.]

Could you please explain the line in the third stanza: "Let purpose guide the little wills of men"?

The stanza begins: "From the centre where the Will of God is known, Let purpose guide the little wills of men." This refers to Shamballa, the earth's highest spiritual centre. It is in etheric matter, and within it sits the Council of the Lord of the World, Sanat Kumara (the Ancient of Days of the Bible). From Shamballa issues the Plan (of evolution of all kingdoms) which embodies the Will and the Purpose of our Planetary Logos, "The Purpose which the Masters know and serve", as the last line of the stanza states.

If the Purpose of God, invoked through the Invocation, guides "the little wills of men" then the little separate wills of men (and of course women) will come at last into correct alignment with the Divine Will and the Plan of Love and Light will work out. All that we do as a race is in response (adequate or inadequate) to the divine energies of Will (or Purpose), Love and Light released into the world by the Spiritual Hierarchy of Masters.

Please explain the meaning of a line in the fourth stanza: "And may it seal the door where evil dwells."

The forces of evil, or darkness on this planet receive their energies from the cosmic astral plane. They are, fundamentally, the forces of materiality, the forces of matter. They are part of the involutionary process of God — God involving Itself in matter and producing the pairs of opposites, Spirit and Matter.

These involutionary forces uphold the matter aspect of the planet. Were they to restrict their activity to that purpose it would be lawful. But when this activity overflows onto the evolutionary arc on which we are, it becomes an evil and is inimical to our spiritual progress. Because they work on the physical plane, the forces of darkness have always had an advantage over the Masters of Wisdom, who represent the forces of light. Since Atlantean times, the Masters have worked on the higher mental planes. So Their hands have been somewhat tied in relation to man's life on the physical plane. However, since 1966, a balance has been achieved, and the forces of light are now stronger in the world. The Masters can now come out into the open and work with humanity on the physical plane. They can add Their power to the existing power of the disciples and of the men and women of goodwill.

The forces of evil on the planet have been defeated but not destroyed. So, "And may it seal the door where evil dwells" refers to the "sealing" energies. Their work is to seal those forces away in their own domain by lifting humanity above the level where we can be influenced. We can then spiritualize matter, which is what we are really here to do.

In the Great Invocation is the phrase: ". . . restore the Plan on Earth." Which Plan? What should be restored?

To quote the Master D.K. (*A Treatise on White Magic*, by Alice A. Bailey): "The Plan as at present sensed, and for which the Masters are steadily working, might be defined as follows: It is the production of a subjective synthesis in humanity and of a telepathic interplay which will eventually annihilate time. It will make available to every man all past achievements and knowledges, it will reveal to man the true significance of his mind and brain, and make him therefore omnipresent and eventually open the door to omniscience. This next development of the Plan will produce in man an understanding — intelligent and co-operative — of the divine purpose for which the One in

Whom we live and move and have our being has deemed it wise to submit to incarnation. Think not that I can tell of the Plan as it truly is. It is not possible for any man below the grade of initiate of the third degree to glimpse it, and far less to understand it. . . . All can therefore strive towards achieving continuity of consciousness and at awakening that inner light which, when seen and intelligently used, will serve to reveal other aspects of the Plan, and especially that one to which the illumined knower can respond and usefully serve."

The last line of the Great Invocation, "May Light and Love and Power restore the Plan on Earth", implies that at some point in the past the Plan was manifest on Earth. Was this the case, and if so, when?

The Plan is considered by the Hierarchy to have been manifesting, more or less correctly, during the period from middle to late Atlantean times, that is, up until around 100,000 years ago. That was a time, however, when the Masters of that period worked openly in the world, thus able to influence and guide humanity directly. With the externalization of Their work now (that is what the reappearance of the Christ and the Masters actually entails) the Plan will once again be restored, this time with the conscious participation of humanity.

I respect Maitreya very much but why should we visualize an inverted Y-shaped table when saying the stanza of the Great Invocation that begins: "From the point of Love . . .". Why inverted? Wouldn't it make more sense to leave the Y the right way up? I know something about Runes, and the upside down Y makes me think of the YN Rune which is the Power of the Earth. While I really want to be involved in the Transmission work, your answer to this question is very important to me.

In visualizing the inverted Y-shaped table, you are connecting with something which already exists. The Masters sit at such a table with the Three Great Lords, the Christ, the Manu and the

Lord of Civilization, at the three points of what, energetically, is really an equilateral triangle of tremendous power. The Christ stands at the apex of the triangle, hence the *inverted* Y.

(1) A friend of mine has trouble in using the word "Christ" in the Great Invocation because it reminds her of the picture the churches have painted of Him. Is it therefore possible to say "love" instead of "Christ"? (2) Also, can't we leave out the sentence, "and may it seal the door where evil dwells"? Evil sounds too negative, and furthermore it will disappear automatically when love wins.

(1) This seems to be quite a common problem. However, the Great Invocation has been translated into terms we can understand by Hierarchy and should *not* be changed. While Maitreya embodies the energy of love, the words "love" and "the Christ" are not the same nor do they have the same associations on a mass scale. (2) Likewise, it is important *not* to change the sentence about sealing "the door where evil dwells". Evil exists and its exponents, the Lords of Materiality, *must* be sealed off to their own domain — the upholding of the matter aspect of the planet. This is done by lifting humanity, through the agency of the Christ and the Masters, above the level where they can be influenced, as now, by these destructive forces. The present focus of these forces is *commercialization* which, Maitreya warns, is a major threat to our well-being. Evil does not "disappear automatically when love wins". With respect, that is sentimentality. The forces of evil can only be restrained to their own domain when people everywhere recognize the difference between materialistic abundance in response to market forces and true, spiritual sufficiency. This is a hard lesson for (especially) the developed nations to learn.

Now that the Christ is in the world, should the wording of the Great Invocation be changed?

No. I know that some groups have changed the line, "May Christ return to earth", to "Christ has returned to earth" or something similar. This change is a mistake and does not proceed from Hierarchy. As I have already explained, "May Christ return to earth" refers not only to Maitreya, the Christ, but to the Hierarchy of which He is the head. This line should be maintained as given to invoke the group of Masters (some 40 in all) Who will return to the outer world over the next 20 years or so.

For years, several groups have disliked the line, "And may it seal the door where evil dwells", and have changed it. Again, this is a mistake. The wording of this Invocation has been most carefully worked out by Hierarchy as a form — which we can use and understand — of the deeply occult mantram used by Maitreya.

Some individuals and groups claim to have 'received' new forms of the Great Invocation, presumably from Hierarchy. I believe this to be nothing other than the result of glamour. As humanity fits itself for their reception and use, there will be released eventually, new, more esoteric forms of this invocation. But, as yet, they have not even been formulated by the Masters. They must relate to the state of being of humanity at the time and this is still unknown.

Should the Great Invocation be said at the beginning or at the end of the meditation?

It should be said at the beginning. An invocation is used to invoke or call forth energy. You invoke the energy, then transmit it. There are many groups who use the Great Invocation at the end of their meditation as a kind of blessing. This is nice, but it is not potent. The Invocation is an *invocation*. You invoke the energy from the Buddha, the Christ and Shamballa, then send it out to the world. This Invocation never fails. Focus the attention high and hold it there. If your physical brain is thus correctly aligned, the energy will flow.

Can we use the Great Invocation as an inner prayer, along with, for example, the Lord's Prayer, or would we disturb the Masters if we do that?

It is not given as an inner prayer but rather as an invocation of the energy of Hierarchy. Nevertheless, its use would not, I am sure, disturb the Masters.

Is there a correct way to sound the Great Invocation?

The Great Invocation is so powerful a mantram and so broad in its margin of error that it can be said perfectly, semi-perfectly or very inadequately and it will still invoke the energies, as long as you say it with intention. You have to bring the will into it. When you say it, your attention must be focused at the ajna centre between the eyebrows. It is the intention of the will linked with Hierarchy that does it. And it should be said aloud.

I belong to a Transmission Meditation group which started three years ago. Lately the Great Invocation has been omitted at the start of the Transmission. When I asked why I was told that the Masters now know we meet at this time and place. Do we still need to recite the Invocation?

Yes. Every group, no matter how long it has been in existence, should use the Invocation. Of course the Masters know that the group meets at that time and place but there is value for the people involved in saying the Invocation. Apart from anything else, it strengthens their subjective link with Hierarchy.

Chapter III

How to Form a Transmission Group

What are the prerequisites for forming a Transmission group?

One is a desire to serve the world — a simple, altruistic motive of serving. It is not the place to seek individual guidance, contact with the astral planes or messages of any kind. It is simply a giving of oneself in service, acting as a positive mental channel through which the energies sent by the Masters can be stepped down.

Another requirement is regularity and continuity. The group should always meet at the same place and time every week. The Masters need to know that every Monday for instance, at a certain location, at eight o'clock in the evening, or whenever, they will find a group of individuals ready and willing to transmit the energies.

The Christ said in Palestine: "Where two or three are gathered together in My name, there I am." That is literally true in the energetic sense. Where two or three are gathered together in the name of the Masters (or the Christ as the Head of the Masters) to transmit energy, that energy will flow. Individually you could do it, but the beauty of group formation is that more energy can safely be put through a group than through separate individuals.

In London we meet three times a week and transmit for many hours, seldom for less than four. We make it a rule that people arrive at eight and then they can leave whenever they wish. When they leave, they go quietly without disturbing those who stay longer. Do not finish at a certain time at the behest of the least concentrated, or the one who has to leave the soonest. Start together and finish when the energy flow ceases. However, free will must not be violated, so no one is compelled either to attend the group or to attend regularly. Gradually you will find

35

that you begin to love it, and to look forward to that day. You put that day aside. Whatever else you have to do is secondary because that is your Transmission night. Again, the prerequisites are service, regularity, continuity, and commitment. You have to be committed.

Please describe step by step how to conduct a Transmission Meditation in my home.

All you need is the desire to serve and some friends who wish to do likewise. Together, arrange a time and place at which to meet regularly. You might also invite someone from an existing group to an inaugural meeting. This person could go through the procedures with your group.

You need to learn the Great Invocation so that you can say it as a group. Many groups also use tapes of the Christ's messages. Between 6 September 1977 and 27 May 1982, at my public meetings in London, the Christ gave a series of 140 messages to the world through me. In them He releases fragments of His teachings and seeks to evoke from His listeners the desire to share and to make His presence known. At the time the messages were given, tremendous energies were released which were magnetized onto the tapes. Each time these cassettes are played the energy is re-released. This raises the consciousness of the groups who use these messages. Those who do not have cassettes may read one or two of the Messages together aloud before the Transmission. This has the same effect of invoking the energy from Hierarchy. It is impossible, I believe, to read these messages aloud with serious intent without invoking the energy from the Christ.

Then you sound aloud the Great Invocation in a focused and attentive state. As soon as you do that, you make a telepathic link with the Hierarchy of Masters. While saying the Great Invocation or the Christ Messages, you should hold your attention at the ajna centre between the eyebrows. This is the directing centre. Hold it there without any kind of strain during the Transmission. It is very simple. Raise your attention until it is behind the eyebrows.

You will find that your attention may drop down to the solar plexus centre. Your mind will wander. As soon as you realize that your attention is wandering, silently sound OM and your focus will come back automatically to the centre between the eyebrows. Every time your mind wanders off, silently sound OM. Do not meditate on the OM but use it to bring your attention back. Keep your eyes closed while meditating because it is much easier, then, to hold your attention on the ajna centre.

Throughout the Transmission Meditation the holding of your attention behind the eyebrows ensures a mental focus. Do not become negative and passive but hold a very focused mental *positive* position. You will find that the energies themselves hold your attention up. Time goes very fast; an hour will seem like fifteen minutes. Indeed, you will lose all sense of time. It is important to be relaxed, both physically and mentally. That is all you need do. The Masters do the real work.

It is not a part of Their plan that you transmit these energies to any particular person, group or country. For example, someone might think: "There's a terrible situation going on in the Middle East," and that he should direct his thought to that area during Transmission. This is not what is required. Only the Masters know on a scientific basis, what energies, in what potencies, in what balance are needed in any particular place at any particular time.

Once the group is established, the Masters know exactly who you are and where you are. They see you clairvoyantly. They then send the energies through the group. It is a highly scientific process. They know what that group can take. They know which particular rays or types of energy make up the group, which rays are governing the individuals, and the manipulation of energy is in accordance with that fact. Some people will take one set of energies and some another. In this way the Masters can pour Their energy into the world. They need such transformers to do it.

What exactly do you mean by "aligning the physical brain with the soul"?

Sooner or later we have to come into a state of alignment between the physical brain and the soul. That is what meditation does. By meditation you gradually build a channel called the "antahkarana", which is a channel of light from the physical plane up to the soul. Simultaneously, the soul is building the same bridge down toward the physical. This channel, when formed, provides a link between the soul and its vehicle, and vice versa. This is the process whereby the man or woman gradually becomes at-one with the soul. The soul 'grips' the vehicle and reflects itself through it. By the use of the mantram OM and the holding of the attention at the ajna centre between the eyebrows, an alignment is created between the brain and soul.

How important is alignment to Transmission Meditation?

Very important. It is the alignment between the brain and the soul which allows the Masters, working from the soul level, to channel the energies through the groups.

[*Editor's note*: See Chapter IX, "Maintaining Alignment", for further discussion on the importance of alignment.]

Are there any special breathing techniques we should use during Transmission Meditation?

No. The breathing should be natural, light, high in the chest and silent. With experience you will find that the breathing becomes so light it practically stops for quite long periods. These are often ended with a sudden, strong 'gasp' of air intake.

Is Transmission Meditation working whether we feel it or not?

If you are aligned, yes. The Transmission is coming mainly from the Buddhic level. It is stepped down for us by the Masters and we step it down further. Alignment is necessary to transmit it.

Please explain the difference between using OM inwardly and sounding it aloud.

If you sound OM aloud, you ground the energy on the physical plane. If you say it inwardly you are placing it on the upper levels of the astral plane, and if you think it, you place it on the mental plane.

The planes are states of consciousness, energies vibrating at certain points that make us aware. We have physical plane consciousness; therefore the physical plane is a reality. We have astral (emotional) plane consciousness; and so the astral plane is a reality. We have, more-or-less, mental plane consciousness; therefore the lower levels of that are a reality to humanity. The higher plane is always more powerful than the lower. People think that the physical plane is the plane where everything happens, but actually the physical plane is the least powerful plane on which the energies operate. The OM correctly sounded inwardly is actually more powerful than correctly sounded on the physical. It does more at a higher level.

At the beginning of the meeting, you may wish to sound OM aloud in unison. That will immediately raise the vibration of the room. (If you are in a room in which you have an on-going Transmission group, you do not need to do this.)

When you sound OM aloud, you are really saying A–U–M; as you say A, it is vibrating at the base of the spine; as you say U, it is vibrating in the heart centre, or between the solar plexus and the heart, depending on who you are; and when you say the M, it is vibrating in the head. If you say AUM you are bringing all three vibrations together from the base of your spine to the top of your head. That is the power of the AUM. The inward-sounding of the OM is used not to ground energy, but simply to help send the energy into the world. The OM is used to put our attention at the mental plane level where the energy can then go out. If our attention is focused down at the solar plexus, then the energy goes out into the world on the astral plane and all our astral thoughtforms will discolour these spiritual energies which we transmit. As your attention wanders off, sound OM inwardly to bring your attention back to the mental plane.

Isn't there a danger of creating an hypnotic state in continually sounding OM if one has difficulty in concentrating?

You do not sound OM continually but only to bring the attention back to the ajna centre (between the eyebrows) when it wanders off. In practice, you will find that the energies themselves help to keep the attention up.

Can the method of the 'Sacred Presence in ourselves' in the heart, for example, replace the repetition of OM?

For some people, yes. The problem is that people in general are unaware of their point in evolution or the correct method of meditation at that point. It is safer and usually more valuable to focus attention on the ajna centre and sound OM to hold it there. This is the heart centre in the head, the directing centre, and its use shifts the focus onto the mental plane.

Is it better to use OM during Transmission Meditation rather than your own mantram?

I would advise confining the use of your own meditation technique, whatever it involves, to that meditation, which would normally be 20 minutes or half an hour, twice a day. During a Transmission Meditation on the other hand, use OM. Most meditations using a mantram are ingoing meditations, but Transmission work is a very light kind of meditation — it does not involve going in at all. So I would separate the two. You will find that by the stimulus of the centres the Transmission work will enhance the personal meditation.

Can mantrams produce bad effects if not sounded correctly?

Yes. Mantrams produce their effects in relation to the advancement (that is, state of consciousness) of the user. The more advanced the user of the mantrams, the more powerful and the more correct the effects. The use of mantrams, however, can have a mere hypnotizing effect.

My children, who are four and two years old, say OM when they meditate because they imitate their parents. Is this dangerous?

No. Children sounding OM do so at such an ineffective level that there is nothing to fear.

Is there not a danger in transmitting these energies? What about for children and for pregnant women?

There is a danger inherent in all meditation, of course. These are very powerful forces. The forces which you receive from your soul during meditation are very powerful, especially if you meditate in a dynamic fashion. Transmission Meditation is a very dynamic meditation, although it is also the simplest one I know. But it is totally under the control of the Masters. They are experts and will not send through your centres more energy than you can safely take.

The only provision is that no children under the age of 12 should take part in a Transmission Meditation for the simple reason that the force centres, the chakras, of a child under the age of 12 are still relatively unformed and unstable, so the energy could do them harm. It is also not advised to keep infants or babies in the same room where Transmission Meditation is taking place. The Masters have to shield them from the energies and it is a waste of Their valuable energies to do so.

It is safe for pregnant women, if they are healthy and the pregnancy is normal. In fact, babies in the womb seem to like Transmission energies. They often start kicking during Transmission.

Is Transmission Meditation to be done only by mentally stable and well-anchored people?

41

Transmission Meditation should be done, in principle, only by mentally stable and well-anchored people. In specific cases it can benefit somebody who does not necessarily fit into these categories, but in general when people are in a highly unbalanced emotional state or in a psychotic condition, they should not take part in Transmission work. The energies are too high and there is a danger of over-stimulation.

(1) As a schizophrenic patient I have come into contact with your work. My question is whether it would be beneficial for me to join a Transmission Meditation group? (2) I would like to find some form of service to be of some use to society as a whole. I am on medication to control my condition. Have you any general advice for people suffering from similar psychological conditions?

(1) No. It could be over-stimulating and create problems. (2) Find some more *exoteric* field of service in which powerful energies are not involved. For example Oxfam, Greenpeace, Friends of the Earth, etc., etc.

Since it is not everyone's cup of tea to take part in a Transmission group, how do you know whether you are fit or not?

Only by practice. It is really a process of self-selection. You go to a Transmission group or form a group, and do it a few times and either you are attracted by it and find it useful, satisfying and really rather pleasurable, or you find it such a terrible bore that you never go back. There is no glamour, there is nothing to talk about, there are no stories, no gurus, no devotion. It is a purely objective, scientific process; it is work, a job. You can do it in any degree of intensity — up to three times a week, for three or four hours. Of course, not everyone can maintain that intensity or rhythm — and so it tends to be a self-selective process. Those who cannot do it keep away. Those for whom it is natural tend to be the ones who do it.

This is an act of service. It is service given to you 'on a plate'. Many people today want to serve. People say: "I long to serve but I don't know how to begin." Well, there is a world to save. There are millions of people starving in the world. There are countless millions who are poverty-stricken, and so on. There is a whole world to change and save and transform. So you do not have to go further than next door to serve. You do not have to go further than your Transmission room to serve. It is service given to you; the simplest, easiest form of service that exists. I can vouch for its effectiveness and its simplicity, but it is not for everyone, because some people want more. They want to have something to talk about: "Where am I? Who am I? Does my guru love me, does he not love me? Is he a higher or a lower guru? Is he bigger or lesser than so-and-so? Did you get that marvellous feeling when he looked at you?" and so on. There is none of that in Transmission work — it is a pure act of service to the world, and so it tends to be self-selecting.

If a person is closed to esotericism can the energetic contact (in Transmission Meditation) be established?

Most certainly. This is a scientific process and is not dependent on 'belief' or academic knowledge.

I've been doing Zen practice (hara-focus) most of my adult life, and Transmission Meditation (ajna-focus) for a dozen years. I believe you said that full-time ajna-focus is the method for making/maintaining soul-contact. Does this mean one ought to give up zazen and full-time Zen practice in favour of the ajna-focus if one hopes to evolve into stabilized soul-contact?

In general, yes, although much depends on the individual. Any meditation is a method, more or less scientific, depending on the meditation, of making and deepening soul contact. For most aspirants and disciples of today, however, the ajna focus is the prescribed one. This creates an alignment between the personality and the soul essential to the ultimate at-one-ment of these two aspects of ourselves. Eventually, the ajna centre acts as the synthesizer of the energies of all the centres below it.

If our chakras are insufficiently opened (because of karmic reasons) can Transmission Meditation (1) provoke an amelioration of our general state; (2) lead to an aggravation of our problems; (3) be inefficient; (4) lead to a distortion of these energies; (5) in short, should we and can we all transmit?

(1) Yes. (2) No. (3) Yes. (4) No. (5) Yes. The whole process is highly scientific and under the control of Master scientists.

Is it necessary to have reached a certain level to profit by and serve through Transmission Meditation?

There is a self-selecting process at work in that only those sufficiently evolved to *want* to serve will be attracted to Transmission Meditation. But that provision aside, no special expertise or experience is required to transmit the Hierarchical energies in this way.

Are there moods or mental states which prevent one from having useful Transmissions?

Yes. Conditions of anguish, anger (especially anger), fear — in other words, strong, emotional, astral reactions are not conducive to the kind of soul alignment which is necessary for the Transmission. On the other hand, if you can make the alignment despite the emotional disturbance, you will find that the spiritual energies will be very conducive to neutralizing that state of mind.

What is the significance of coming together physically to transmit the energy, rather than mentally connecting with other people as in Triangles meditation?

44

Masters use groups because more energy can be safely passed through a group and at a higher potency than through the same number of separate individuals.

The aim is to form a Transmission group through which X plus some factor of energy can be sent rather than just X through separate individuals. For example, if one person were in New Jersey, another in New York, and I were in London, and we did not know each other but were all acting as transmitters of energy, the Masters could send through each of us a certain amount of energy, whatever our centres could stand. But if we were to come together as a group, we would create a triangle. The Masters would send the energy through that triangle which would potentize the energy. It would not be simply one plus one plus one. It would be one plus one plus one plus a factor of potentization by the circulation of energy around the centres of all three of us. When you have a group of more than three, there are multiple numbers of such triangles which then create other geometrical formations. It is an enormously complicated science — complicated geometrical formations utilizing the centres of the individuals in the group.

There are important added factors on many levels in the physical coming together of the group. It also adds a dimension of vitality to the Transmission which would otherwise be lacking. It adds a dimension to the identity of the group as a group. It contributes to the growth of the group soul which is a long-term process. It creates a bond of love among the group members, which is of course the best thing you can do for yourself and the group. It is very important to come together in this way, from the energetic and psychological point of view, for the nurturing of the group as a unit of consciousness and as a vehicle for the Love of the Christ, now and in the coming time.

If a Transmission group member cannot attend on a particular occasion, can he or she 'plug into' the group?

If a member cannot attend for an important reason then he or she can mentally link up with the group. Visualize the group sitting in its usual place. Visualize the individual members of the group and see yourself sitting as a member of that group. When you say the Great Invocation you will find that you are linked to the Transmission and the group will proceed almost as if you were there. But you should not do it too often. It is difficult to form a group identity when you only occasionally meet each other.

If only two people are interested in forming a Transmission group, what should we do?

Then you will have Transmission Meditation with two people. It is possible to do Transmission by yourself also. But, of course, only so much energy can be placed through one person, or through two people. Being a triangle potentizes the energies out of all recognition.

You may mentally link up with other groups which are meeting at the same time. There are Transmission groups now over much of the world. Transmission is fundamentally taking place on the soul level. Whenever and wherever you are doing it, you will be linked into a chain of light which is being formed by the Christ and the Masters throughout the world on the soul level.

Are three people sufficient for a Transmission Meditation group or should we aim for more?

Three constitutes a triangle and therefore a potentization of the energies sent, and is the basic unit, but the group should be expanded if possible. More energy can safely be sent through a greater number of transmitters. In short, the more the better.

The following example will show clearly how important it is for each member to always attend Transmission Meditation meetings. A group of three people will make one triangle and four people will make four triangles. Five people will create 10 triangles, six make 20 triangles, seven make 35, eight will make

56, nine will make 84, 10 will make 120, and so on. Therefore, the larger the number of people in a group, the more potently the group can work. By the same token, every member who either leaves early or does not attend, weakens the power of the group dramatically. Each person's participation is therefore very valuable.

[*Editor's note:* Column A represents the number of people in a Transmission group; Column B indicates the number of triangular relationships resulting. Column C shows the number of triangles that will be lost when the current number of people is reduced by one (when one person leaves the Transmission).]

A	B	C	A	B	C
10	120	36	90	117,480	3,916
20	1,140	171	100	161,700	4,851
30	4,060	406	110	215,820	5,886
40	12,000	741	120	280,840	7,021
50	19,600	1,176	130	357,760	8,256
60	34,220	1,711	140	447,580	9,591
70	54,740	2,346	150	551,300	11,026
80	82,160	3,081	200	1,313,400	19,701

What guidelines should we use in letting people join our Transmission group?

I believe that all groups should be open. That is not to say that you should suffer fools or those who would break up the group, but it is so boring for that type of person that they do not come anyway. It is just work. It is not easy sitting and concentrating, and you do concentrate, even if it is only on the ajna centre, for many hours. It is difficult to say to people: "No, you can't come into this group." However, like attracts like. When someone comes in who is incompatible he tends not to stay, because if you work intensely and with concentration, the rhythm is usually too strong for the person who does not have the concentration.

But for those who do stay on, you have to get over personality differences.

I recommend that you leave the group as open as possible; that if people want to come, let them come, even if it is not every single time. If they come sometimes and get something from it and do not disrupt the group, I would let it go at that. It is very important not to infringe free will. You have to do this from your own free will. It is service and you cannot bully people into service. From time to time, without any kind of pressure, you can make it known that it is a good thing to come as often as possible, but you have to leave it to them. I would also encourage people to bring friends along if they have done meditation and if they seem sympathetic.

An important thing is that people should have the sense that they can leave the group at any time and not take any further part in it. They should also have the option of leaving the meditation itself at whatever time they wish.

I have heard from a friend that there is a Transmission group here in Belgium in which the 'leader' is putting pressure on people to stay in his group even if they wish to leave. He more or less threatens them with bad karmic consequences if they leave. I think this is not right. What is your opinion about this?

This, if true, is a serious breach of the law of free will. No one should ever be pressured or emotionally blackmailed into attending Transmission groups. There are too many so-called new age organizations which employ these questionable methods to keep adherents.

Recently, I tried to join a Transmission group, the name and address of which were mentioned in Share Nederland. The people there told me that they could not let me in, because, according to them, I am not experienced enough to do this type of meditation. Have you authorized groups to judge about applicants' capability to undertake Transmission Meditation? Would they be so evolved as to be able to know?

No, I have not authorized anyone to make such a judgment. I always present Transmission Meditation as a form of service open to anyone over the age of 12, needing no previous experience or expertise. Of course, any group has the right to exclude those they might think to be not compatible. Perhaps this was the case here and has been wrongly interpreted.

How long should we transmit?

Groups vary enormously in the length of time they sit in Transmission Meditation — from half an hour to five, six or seven hours, once, twice or three times a week. I know groups who start at 7:00 and finish at 7:30; then they have tea and cakes and chat, and they are very proud to be a Transmission group, half an hour per week. Some think they have to start at a certain time and finish at a certain time, all together. This is not the case. It is important and useful that a group starts the Transmission Meditation at the same time, but there is no reason at all why the length of the Transmission should be regulated by the concentration ability of the weakest member. Many group leaders have said to me: "But they won't sit longer; they get tired after an hour; they want to go home or have tea." So it should be open. Those who wish to stay longer should be able to stay longer and those who want to go can go.

The greater the number in the group the more the energy can be potentized. The energy is not sent individually through the members of the group. If you have three people, that makes up a triangle; if you have six people, that makes several triangles, and it is through these triangular formations, which can be expanded to stars and various geometric shapes, that the Masters send the energy. Obviously, every time someone leaves the group to go home, the group is weakened. But it is still better for the Transmission to go on with fewer people for a longer time than for the whole group to go on for a very short time.

I know that people sometimes have to come long distances, and that they want to get together socially afterwards, so they want to keep the Transmission work short. But it is more important to give time to the Transmission than to chat with the group. That may be pleasant but it is not service, and Transmission work is service. But everyone has the total right to leave the group meeting quietly at any time and let the others carry on.

I would suggest one hour as a minimum, aiming to increase gradually to three or four hours, or for as long as the energies flow.

Since we have increased the length of our Transmission Meditation (and decided to have it open-ended instead of drinking tea after Transmission), a lot of our group have stopped taking part in the Transmissions. Is it better, therefore, to restart shorter Transmissions, and maybe attract them once more to the Transmission work?

Why not invite everyone to a discussion of this problem? Surely some kind of compromise between open-ended Transmissions and socializing can be worked out among you.

I hold a Transmission Meditation group in my house. When the others leave can I continue transmitting on my own after I have shown them out, or do you need three people to go on?

Sometimes one is left alone, and that is all right. You sit as long as the energies flow. But why do you have to get up to show them out? Let them find their own way out!

Is it possible to participate in a Transmission group in a dream state?

No. It is possible to take part in a Transmission Meditation and to fall asleep. If you are nodding for only a few seconds, the Transmission still goes on. But when people actually fall asleep, they are not taking part in the Transmission, no matter what they may dream. A dream is an activity of the astral and the lower mental planes. The Transmission is taking place on the higher mental level.

But people do fall asleep during Transmission Meditation. It happens all the time, in all groups. Some sleep for a little while, and some spend most of the time asleep. The energies — because of their potency and people's unfamiliarity with them — knock them out, so to speak. But they gradually get used to the energies. It becomes less and less necessary for them to fall asleep, especially if they choose a day when they are not too tired. Holding the attention high is tiring if you have not done it before, but for anyone who has meditated somewhat, it is not so difficult. You will find that the energies themselves help you concentrate.

Is it possible to meditate with success lying down?

It is possible but to my mind not the best position for meditation. It is too easy to fall asleep!

Why must we always transmit at night and not in the morning when we are at our best?

Most Transmission groups meet at night since most people work during the day. But there is nothing to prevent anyone doing the Transmission work in the morning. The energies of the Hierarchy are available at all times. They never shut up shop.

Why must we transmit in the dark? It is so easy to go to sleep.

Of course it is not necessary to transmit in the dark. The point is that most people can concentrate better in a subdued light. There is no other reason why you should not transmit in broad daylight, as we often do during Transmission Meditation workshops.

In Transmission Meditation, instead of verbal instructions by one person during the meditation, is it acceptable to ring a bell to refocus the attention?

If it is acceptable to those present it is acceptable, but to my mind it is not a very good idea. The verbal reminder to keep the focus at the ajna centre works because of the specific reference to the centre. There is no such association with a bell sound. I believe people would quickly become used to the bell and ignore it — or even not hear it.

Is it possible to change your venue after some time if it isn't possible to carry on?

Yes. The essential thing about Transmission Meditation is its regularity, that you be at the same time, the same day, the same place every week, whether that is once or twice or three times a week so that the Masters will know that They will find a group ready to be used as channels for Their energies. Once the group is formed, the Masters know the individuals connected with it. They can see you clairvoyantly. They see exactly the state of the centres, chakras, the light that each individual and therefore each group radiates, and They can find you. But I think you should not change the venue every week. Give Them a chance!

Is it possible to have a break during the Transmission?

It is perfectly permissible to take a break for a few minutes if you like, and then transmit again.

If a new group starts does the Master need to be informed about it?

The Master does not need to be informed of anything. Groups automatically receive the energies when they sound the Great Invocation. The Great Invocation is given to invoke these energies; that is what it is for. But if a new group is formed in the United States, for example, you should inform Tara Center.

Then they know that you are on the network and when someone rings them and says: "I am in Arkansas and I am looking for a Transmission group", they can inform him of any groups on their list which are in his area.

CHAPTER IV

EXPERIENCES DURING TRANSMISSION

As you are sitting in the Transmission Meditation group stepping down the energy, do you experience physical sensations?

It depends on who you are. Most people have a strong physical experience of the energy in the etheric body, which is of finer, more subtle matter than the dense physical body. People may experience it as hot and cold vibrations in the etheric. They may, if they are sensitive, experience the energy in a particular chakra, the heart or the throat for example. Not everyone has this sensitivity to vibration. Some people say they do not actually feel the energies. They know they are there, they experience them in some way, but they do not feel them. They say: "I don't know when it starts or when it stops, I rely on other people to tell me." But by their reactions I can tell that they do know when they start or cease.

One man in our group hears the energies. As I say which energy is coming, he hears a different note. Another person sees constant changing waves of colour. So there are different ways to experience them. It depends on your own particular type of response to vibration — mental, visual, auditory or sensory. I myself feel it so strongly that I find it difficult to understand why other people do not, but I know they do not. Some people have that kind of physical body — they are simply not aware of energy changes or of the vibration of the etheric centres.

Why is it that during Transmission Meditation sometimes the energies seem very powerful indeed, and at other times you feel much less or nothing at all?

A remarkable wisp of light can be seen in the left of the photograph. In this case, spiritual energy, coming through the people and then transmitted through the tetrahedron, has become visible.

It may be that at the particular time when you are feeling nothing, the energies which are being sent through the other members of the group are not going through you because they are not your particular line. Groups are made up of people of different ray lines or types of energies.

There are seven major rays which stem from seven stars in the Great Bear, and each of us is on one of these rays. The ray of our soul, the Higher Self, will be the same throughout our existence. The personality ray can change from life to life.

The 1st ray is the ray of Will, or Power, or Purpose; the 2nd is the ray of Love-Wisdom; the 3rd, the ray of Active Intelligence, Higher Mind; the 4th is the ray of Harmony through Conflict, or Beauty; the 5th, that of Lower Mind or Concrete Science; the 6th is the ray of Abstract Idealism or Devotion; and the 7th, which is the ray coming into force now in this new age, is the ray of Ceremonial Order, or Magic, or Ritual, or Organization. We are all of us on one of these rays, as souls and as personalities. Our mental bodies, our emotional bodies and our physical bodies are also each on one of these rays. Nations have souls and personalities just as human beings do and are also on these rays, both as souls and as personalities.

The Masters are in control of all the rays. There are seven major ashrams or groups in the Hierarchy, with a Master at the head of each, and there are 42 subsidiary ashrams stemming from these seven major ones — 49 ashrams altogether. Each line of seven is governed by, and utilizes the energy of, one of these seven rays. In Transmission groups people will tend to be of one of two ray structures, the 2-4-6 line or the 1-3-5-7 line. If, for example, you are a 2nd-ray soul with a 2nd-ray personality, then it is quite possible that the 1st and 7th ray energies will be flowing at a particular time through some members of the group, but you will not be receiving them. You will experience a hiatus at that time. Then the energy will flow again but it will be your line this time, the 2-4-6 line.

It may be that at the time you feel nothing you are unaligned or just so tired that you do not respond to the vibration. There are also peaks and troughs in the sending of the energies themselves. In addition, very high energies may be beyond your range of feeling because they come no lower than the higher mental planes. People respond very differently. But the fact that you do not feel anything does not mean that you are not transmitting energy.

[*Editor's note*: For more information on the seven rays, see *Maitreya's Mission*, Vols. I and II, by Benjamin Creme.]

Often, during Transmission Meditation, I see very bright, luminous colours, usually blue or purple, sometimes gold. Could you please say what this signifies?

They are visual manifestations of the energies transmitted during the Meditation.

Why do people have the experience that the Transmission energy is different on different nights?

I think there are two factors here. One is that the energies themselves may be different, have different qualities which have a different effect on you. The other is that people vary from evening to evening because of work patterns or pressure of the atmosphere; they are more or less tired, more or less vitalized, and therefore probably absorb, when the vitality is low, less of the energies than at other times. The energy potential is exactly in proportion to the spiritual tension. Obviously, people who are more advanced in evolution will absorb and transmit energy of higher potency than those who are less evolved. They have greater spiritual tension.

Our own spiritual tension varies from day to day. So, in the same way, we will receive a particular potency of the energy one day, and more or less on another day. The group tension is made up of the sum total of the individual tensions.

In addition, the energies themselves are sent and are brought down by the Masters to different levels. The energy one night may not seem strong at all, not because it is not being sent out powerfully, but because it is not being received sensitively. It may be so high that the apparatus of the group members cannot sense it. The same energy brought down onto a lower plane they feel strongly because they are sensitive to it at the lower level. The lower the plane the more we feel the energy. We only think of what we feel strongly as being strong, but that is dependent on our instrument. It is not usually to do with the strength or otherwise of the energy, although it may be.

Do some of the physical reactions during Transmission Meditation, like coughing, mean there is a blockage in our physical body?

Yes, they usually do. During Transmission Meditation many individuals get a strong tickle in the throat causing them to cough. It happens in all groups. It is a stimulation of the throat centre caused by the incoming energies. There is a block in the flow of the energy through the throat centre, and the best thing is to have a little glass of water under your chair and take a drink.

Also check whether the throat is tense. If it is, visualize the centre and eject the energy from it. Visualize a channel coming out from the centre and, as it were, empty it. Draw the energy from behind the back of the neck through the throat centre and out the front to clean the blockage out.

What causes a blockage in an energy centre?

The energy centres are in the etheric body, a counterpart of the physical body. They are attached to the channel in the centre of the spine (the sushumna) and go through to the front like two cones of energy meeting at the spine. The energies come in one side and out the other, but it is a moving stream and not fixed. If the energy is dammed up it will produce an inflammation, a stasis. If, for example, the muscles of the throat are contracted by the non-use of the energy flowing from the soul through the throat centre, then you can get a blockage of the throat centre.

Those who meditate inevitably invoke energy from the soul. You build the antahkarana, the channel to the soul, and through that channel the energy from the soul flows into the various bodies — mental, astral, and physical — and if it is not used by the disciple in service activity, it gets dammed up in the centres. You might say: "Well, I'm serving, I'm serving 20 hours a day", but do you serve along the right lines? Is it along your own line of least resistance? Do you serve in such a way that you are using the energy, not just trying, but actually using it? Are you, for instance, serving in a physical sense when you should really be serving through the written or spoken word? There are different types of service and you have to use every part of yourself. Some people will be better at one aspect and some at another, but it is the use in a balanced way of all the energies entering from the soul which prevents those blockages.

When I'm concentrating on something in my daily life, I sometimes feel a tingling in the top of my head or feel as if energy is entering me. Am I transmitting?

People feel energy coming in spontaneously from time to time. That is usually not a Transmission. What you are really experiencing 99 times out of 100 is the energy from your own soul. The soul exists on its own plane. That is really who we are — souls. Most of the time our soul is turned in meditation towards the Monad, the Spirit aspect. From time to time it turns its attention towards the man or woman in incarnation, its vehicle. When it does that, and especially with a developed person who is engaged in meditation and service, and is an aspirant, disciple, or initiate, it overshadows its reflection. It pours its energy into the vehicle, whether on the mental, the astral, the etheric physical plane, or a combination of all three. Then you get that feeling which is something like a Transmission, but is not. It is the soul, and it really feels quite different from a Transmission. It feels as if you have a cap on your head, and it comes right down to above the eyebrows. It is like a heavy band all around your head, but it is inside. When that happens, you know it is your soul. You learn to feel the differences among vibrations. There are three distinct vibrations — the Ashramic vibration, the Master's vibration, and your soul vibration — and you have to differentiate among them. First you get to know your own soul. It has a specific vibration and it does not feel at all like the feeling in your head during Transmission Meditation.

In Transmission Meditation the energies are put through the chakras by the Masters and you have no hand in it. You are like an instrument with holes in it, and the energy comes through the holes and out into the world transformed, stepped down. So Transmission is quite a different thing from the energy of the soul. You may also feel the energy of the Christ, or the energies of the rays, and they all feel different in your aura, in your etheric centres. As you become more sophisticated in this process you learn to discern the different energies.

I have been experiencing that sensation of the soul stimulus more and more frequently, sometimes during my meditation (personal and Transmission), and often just at random times, and I'm sometimes able to invoke it at will. What exactly does it mean when this occurs, and is there an attitude of mind or visualization to be used at these times?

The soul alternates its attention between the Monad (upward) and its own reflection, the man or woman in incarnation. This occurs cyclically and these cycles vary both individually and during any given life.

There are cycles of intense soul stimulus (in response to meditation and spiritual aspiration and service) and cycles of relative quiet.

There is no special attitude of mind or visualization (except awareness of the event) to be followed at these times.

When I feel very strong energies, for instance when I read the Messages from Maitreya, how can I tell whether it is from the soul, a Master, or dare I hope, Maitreya?

It is impossible to read the Messages from Maitreya, or say them aloud, without invoking His energy. That is one reason why they were given. It is difficult to say about strong energies in general — it is really a matter of experience and discrimination. It is usually more correct to accept that the energy is from one's own soul.

When we do Transmission Meditation, does the thought process stop automatically?

No. The nature of the lower mind is to think; that monkey-mind jumps about all the time. But there are various techniques for slowing the activity of the mind, the best of which is the slowing of the breath. You will find that the breath and the thought come from the same source. As you slow down the breath, you slow down the thought. When you slow down the thought, you slow down the breath. The two processes work together. You do not have to stop thinking in order to transmit energy. All you have to do is to establish an alignment between the physical brain and the soul.

Do our thoughts obscure the channel of alignment during Transmission Meditation?

Yes, but that does not mean to say that if you are thinking you are not transmitting the energies. It is a question of degree. As soon as the alignment between the physical brain and the soul is made, the energy can be transmitted. So all you have to do during Transmission Meditation is to hold the alignment. If you can hold that alignment and talk at the same time, your thoughts have no effect on the energy at all. The concentration needed is really the concentration of holding the alignment, but if the alignment is there all the time, normally, there is no concentration needed to hold it. What does interfere is the direction of the thought. The astral thoughtforms really discolour the energies. The lower mind thinks, but as long as you do not follow or direct the thought, it does not have any great impact on the energy. If you focus the thought on a particular person, or group, or country, you direct the energy to that person, or group or country, which is exactly what is *not* wanted. So the less you think the better, but it does not mean that lower mind activity has any major impact on the energy flow. The point is that perfection is best, but it is not absolutely essential.

What about negative thoughts that come up during Transmission Meditation — do they discolour the transmission energies?

Yes, they certainly do. We discolour the spiritual energies by our astral thoughtforms. Our fears, anxieties, dreams, fantasies — all that discolours the energy. But if our attention is held high, this will not happen. We think such thoughts because we are focused on the solar plexus. These are actually emotional experiences which are reaching the lower levels of the brain as thoughtforms. But if you hold the attention between the eyebrows, without any kind of strain during the Transmission, none of these things will come up onto the brain level. They will remain emotional reactions and you will deal with them sooner or later, but they will not actually surface during the Transmission. That is why it is important to hold your attention up and not become negative. It is a very positive, poised, mental activity.

The tetrahedron instrument is also invaluable because, among other things, it automatically earths astral thoughtforms. [*Editor's note*: For an explanation of the tetrahedron instrument, see pages 73-77.]

Master D.K. warns of the danger of meditating for too long. Transmission Meditation goes on for long hours. Isn't it dangerous?

We have to differentiate between meditating for too long and transmitting for too long. It is of course possible to meditate for too long, that is, meditating in terms of alignment with the soul. There is just so much energy you can take from the soul and then use. If you do not use it you get stasis and inflammation somewhere, and neurosis starts. But you cannot transmit for too long; it is not possible because the Masters control the sending of the energies.

Never have such potencies been so available to the Christ as they are now, and never has the need for the transmission of these energies into the world been as urgent as now. The urgency has invoked the energies. Why limit yourself to half an hour or an hour when you could just as easily go for two hours, three hours or more? We in England go for four hours plus; recently on this tour we have had Transmissions of seven and nine hours, and in Holland, 11 hours. That is tiring, but not too long. There is no possibility of doing harm. The Masters are in charge and determine the duration of the transmission of the energies.

In the Alice Bailey books, Master D.K. does not talk about Transmission work so He is not warning against it. D.K. is warning against the negative state which can develop in meditating too long, and also of the dangers of over-stimulation by soul energy.

I'm concerned about the blank mind, the empty state people fall into when transmitting. D.K. says not to meditate with a blank mind.

I do not say you should make your mind a blank. You should be alert and open. You should consciously hold your attention at the ajna centre. If you do this you may not be thinking at all, but your mind is not blank. In meditation you must learn the difference between the mind which is poised, absolutely alert, totally aware, and the mind which is blank. You may be more poised and aware with thoughts running through your mind than you are with a blank mind. A mind which is not thinking is not the same as a mind which is blank.

If, during Transmission Meditation, one regularly experiences strong and uncomfortable emotions, is it better to discontinue Transmission for a period of time, until perhaps the feelings subside somewhat, or try to continue on as best as possible in the midst of the emotions? Is the stimulation of strong emotions common in Transmission Meditation?

Try to continue until emotional balance is regained. When properly conducted, that is with the attention focused at the ajna centre (between the eyebrows), the upsurge of strong emotion should be rare.

Why do people tend to fall asleep often during Transmission Meditation?

People fall asleep during Transmission for two reasons: because they are tired, and because they do not find it easy to physically absorb these spiritual energies. An incredible stimulus is given to the work of the groups and to the evolution of the individuals in them. They are dealing with energies which, initially, their physical bodies cannot easily accept and hold. There is a time-lag between the sending and reception of the energies and the actual ability of the physical body to absorb them easily. In Transmission Meditation the bodies of the individuals are gradually being tuned so that they can absorb more and more. But while this process is going on they can easily fall asleep.

Can or should you put yourself under self-hypnosis while transmitting or does this work against what is being accomplished?

Some people find it difficult enough to keep awake the whole time during a Transmission without introducing self-hypnosis. What is required is a *positive mental focus* which entails concentration on the ajna centre (between the eyebrows).

Are the visions and messages people seem to get during Transmission Meditation valid?

Many people have said to me: "We had a marvellous Transmission last Friday. All the Masters were there, the energies were beautiful and they gave us wonderful teachings." That is nonsense. It is pure glamour, illusion, and should be eschewed at all costs. If you are doing that, stop. They do not give marvellous teachings during Transmissions. They do not give any teachings at all during Transmissions. They simply transmit the energies through the people in the group. The "teachings" and the "Masters" around them are in the astral imagination of the people. Because a lot of people come into this more esoteric work from the spiritualist movement they think it is the same thing, but it is not. It has nothing to do with the spirit world and nothing to do with the teachers on the astral planes. It is a scientific process whereby the Masters, working from the Buddhic level, can transform Their energies down onto the physical plane.

Could people have contact with 'entities' during Transmission Meditation?

Yes, mediumistic types may allow themselves to hold a passive, negative focus at the solar plexus and so open themselves to contact from astral entities. The danger is inherent in all meditation work, hence the necessity of holding a positive mental focus (at the ajna centre).

Does Transmission Meditation strengthen the intuition like 'regular' meditation?

Most certainly. Every activity (meditation and/or service) which invokes the soul qualities into the personality life strengthens the intuition. Transmission Meditation is a dynamic forcing process by which the nature of the soul is powerfully invoked. During the Transmission, because all the centres are activated and galvanized, your mind becomes incredibly clear and creative. Through the alignment between the physical brain and the soul which is necessary to do the Transmission, the antahkarana — the channel of light between soul and brain — is kept open. Therefore it is easier for the soul to enhance the intuitive ability of the individual.

Also, you do get inspirational activity. Ideas are dropped down from the soul level into the mind of receptive individuals during Transmission. Many people have very good ideas during the Transmission. But that is not the aim. The aim is the act of service by stepping down the energy so that it becomes useful to a broader section of humanity. The real aim, the true motive, is service.

Is it not dangerous to concentrate on the ajna centre? I have heard that concentration on the chakras can be dangerous.

It certainly can be dangerous to concentrate, as many do, on a particular centre, especially on those below the diaphragm. As you concentrate on a centre, the energy follows your thought. This is a fundamental axiom of occultism — that all in the world is energy, and that energy follows thought.

The activity of the centres has to be awakened in the correct sequence for each ray type, and people do themselves much harm from too little knowledge. The aim must always be the lifting of the energy from the centres below the diaphragm to those above it, along with correct balance and alignment of the chakras.

The governing centre for the mental level is the ajna centre, between the eyebrows. As you become focused on the mental level, emotions become governable without repression. The ajna centre acts as the synthesizer of all the chakras below it and it is perfectly safe to concentrate the attention on it. It is the heart centre in the head. Some say: "I always transmit through the heart centre." This is fine. You cannot transmit through the ajna centre without transmitting through the heart centre. During a

Transmission, you can fix your attention on the ajna centre with full confidence.

I tend to keep my attention focused on the ajna centre continuously, even during everyday activities. Is this not dangerous?

This is certainly not dangerous. If you are really holding the attention focused on the ajna centre continuously, then you are well on the way to achieving mental polarization. Check what happens to your attention, however, when you find yourself in a situation which would normally stimulate a strong emotional reaction. Does your attention remain at the ajna centre or has it dropped to the solar plexus?

When I concentrate on the centre between the eyebrows, I feel like I have an eye there. Is this the third eye?

The ajna centre is not the third eye. The third eye is actually inside, while the ajna centre is in front of the head. The third eye is created by the activity of the disciple himself.

The pituitary body which sits behind the bridge of the nose is related to the ajna centre, while the pineal gland in the centre of the head is related to the head centre. Gradually, meditation heightens the activity of both these glands. When the radiance, the light, given off by the pituitary body and the pineal gland expands sufficiently as a result of this heightened activity, a magnetic contact is made between them, the two centres overlap and a field results. The third eye is born there. It gives higher, clairvoyant vision. That is a different thing from the ajna centre itself.

Thus, when you transmit, you are not holding your attention on the third eye at all, but on the ajna centre between the eyebrows. The pressure you may feel is the energy flowing through the centre. That is where you should have your attention all the time. The attention of most people is down in the solar plexus centre, or even lower, but it should actually be at the ajna centre. This is the governing centre. While you are focused there you are in charge of yourself and your thought activity. From there you also control the activity of the solar plexus which is the centre of the emotions. You cannot make any real advance in evolution until you control the activity of that centre.

For three years, I have been a member of a Transmission Meditation group. We meet twice a week for one hour. After the meditation I feel so clear that I don't fall asleep before 3:00 or 4:00 in the morning. As I have to get up again at 5:00, I feel very tired after such a short sleep. This causes problems at my work. Can you give any advice?

This is quite a common problem in Transmission groups. Personally, I cannot go to sleep for some hours after a Transmission. The thing is to make the best use of the time while awake. Take up some work or reading and you will soon relax into sleep. I recommend that you should, if possible, lengthen the Transmission gradually (say add 15 minutes every two or three weeks) until you are doing up to three hours. Then you will probably want to sleep!

CHAPTER V

IMPROVING THE TRANSMISSION

How can we become better transmitters of energy?

The best way to become a better transmitter is to do more Transmission work. It is a self-grooming process. The more you do, the better you become. It is not possible to do it without being transformed by the energies. What is tremendously potent at one time you will not even notice six months later. Your centres are absorbing it and getting used to it. What you notice is the next higher potency. Only by doing Transmission Meditation do you make progress in it.

In your own private soul meditation you also create an alignment. All thoughts and actions directed toward service and helping the planet also bring about the alignment of the soul with the personality. Your aspiration, meditation and service together create the antahkarana or bridge between the soul and personality. Hold your aspiration as high as possible without giving in to despair, negativity or disappointment. You have to approach meditation and service in a detached way.

In all esoteric and discipleship work, you see the world's need, and, insofar as you are able, as objectively and detachedly as possible, you seek to supply the need. The Christ has said: "Take your brother's need as the measure for your actions, and solve the problems of the world." You have to act with objectivity. You see the need and you supply the need. That is all.

As you do Transmission work in a detached way you are helping the world, but you have to do it just like a job. If you feel important and say: "We are potently helping the world", that is a glamour. In everything you do you have to become as objective and detached as possible. As you do this you automatically transmit the energies better and at a higher potency.

What place do self-observation, awareness, and alertness have in Transmission work? Are they important?

Alertness, yes. Self-observation, no, not really. Self-awareness and self-observation are not stressed in Transmission work. Transmission work is service. It is assumed that groups of transmitters are aspirants to discipleship, or disciples. It is taken for granted that they are getting on with their own self-evolution quite apart from the Transmission Meditation. Transmission work is not in place of self-development. They do whatever practices they wish to do to bring that about. It is not something which is stressed in order to be a part of a Transmission group. There is no teaching in a Transmission group. There is no conscious self-development in a Transmission group, although you cannot channel the energies without being transformed. You do need alertness. You need to be able to hold your attention high. That is not difficult; it does not mean a total, unbroken, fixed attention on the sixth or ajna centre, but that you hold your attention there without any kind of strain. If it drops — and you will find it does (your attention will wander) — you then silently sound OM. Self-awareness, self-development and self-observation you practise in your everyday life. Transmission work does not exclude other types of meditation or training and it is something which potentizes any other practice you do.

In a Transmission group, does it matter how you are seated?

Yes and no — it depends on how conscientious you want to be. I form the centre of our Transmission group, and I have on my left the men in the group and on my right the women. It is simply for the convenience of the Masters. It makes no difference to us, but it does to the Masters. Every energy has polarity, a positive and a negative pole. The men carry the positive and the women the negative charge of the energy. It is a profound science. They are not just transmitting through the individuals but in terms of polarities.

In my experience women tend to take certain of the Christ energies better than most men. They are more attuned to the Christ energy. It feels better if the group is balanced in terms of numbers of men and women, but I do not think it makes any difference at all energetically. For example, in America nearly all the groups have more women than men, while in Holland it is the other way around. The energetic difference has to do with the polarities. When you have, for example, nine women and only one man, that man is very busy! He is being the positive pole for nine other points. But the Masters can arrange that. For them it is no problem. If there are more than six or seven people, I suggest that the men and women should be separate. Anything under six or seven, it does not matter how you sit.

Please explain the function of the tetrahedron instrument and how it is different from a pyramid.

The pyramid was an instrument of Atlantean times. It was built specifically to draw astral energy. The aim of Atlantean man was to perfect the astral vehicle, which he has done very well. That instrument was used then to focus astral energy because that was the highest usable energy of the time. Now, by the turn of the spiral upward, we are moving out of that Atlantean phase even though the majority of humanity are still Atlantean in consciousness, still focused on the astral plane. The focus in this coming time will be on the mental plane. The instrument which draws mental energy is the tetrahedron.

It does two things: the quartz crystal in the centre blends the incoming energies, and the magnetic field potentizes them. The sending is never of just one energy but of several. The instrument transforms the energies downward — brings down the voltage just like a transformer in electricity — but potentizes them at that lower voltage. They are sent out through the gold disk into the world, directed, not by us, but by the Masters to

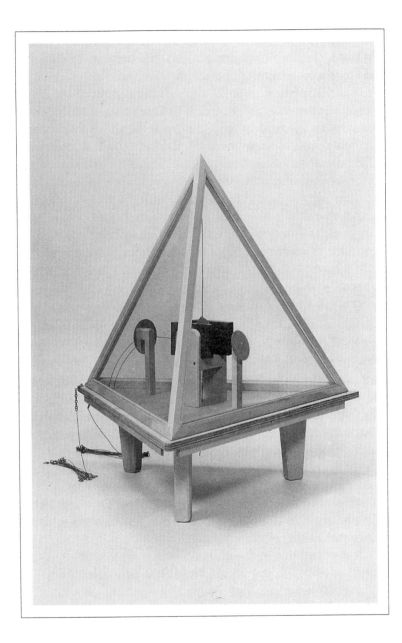

TETRAHEDRON

wherever they are needed, at a voltage that can be used, experienced and assimilated by humanity in general. At the same time it automatically grounds all energy below the mental plane so that the astral thoughtforms of the transmitters do not discolour the spiritual energies.

How much does the tetrahedron instrument improve the Transmission?

The tetrahedron does not itself bring in the energies and it does not in any way improve their reception. It does improve the *transmission* of the energies. These come direct from the Masters to us through the chakras. Then they go from us to the instrument. This instrument is not essential for the work, but it is a useful adjunct. There are only a very few of these instruments in the world and yet there are many Transmision groups and they do just as good work. The tetrahedron further transforms the energies, brings them lower than we can, and at the lowered voltage, it gives them in the end a final boost — potentization.

It also ensures that the energies are sent out on the lower mental plane, which is the plane of the instrument itself. Just by being the shape which it is, it automatically transforms the energies down onto the mental plane. If it were a pyramid, it would transform the energies onto the astral plane, which is not the plane we want to stimulate. In short, it is an adjunct, a benefit for the work, but not essential.

Would it be worthwhile for the Transmission groups to get a tetrahedron?

If they can afford it, yes. It is not essential, but quite important. It is not all that expensive. The larger the group the less expensive it would be per person. It is a very good investment. It would certainly enhance the effectiveness of the group. The only problem with the tetrahedron is the cost, because you need a gold disk of not less than 3.5 inches in diameter weighing not less than 3.5 ounces and a silver disk of not less than 4.5 inches in diameter weighing not less than 4.5 ounces. Twenty-two carat gold will work extremely well, 18 carat will also work well, but less than 18 will not. You lose too many of the higher frequencies or levels of the energies if you use less than 18 carat. Twenty-four is the very best. Of course that is also the most expensive. The rest of the materials, silver wire, magnets, a quartz crystal weighing approximately one kilogram and a glass case, are not very expensive.

There is also something about sitting around an instrument. We have taken part in the Mind-Body-Spirit Festivals every year in London since April 1977, just before Maitreya came into the world, and we always take our tetrahedron to the stall. We have Transmissions every two or three hours and we invite the public to take part in them. People are more interested in the tetrahedron than in the fact that the Christ is in the world. It is more real to them. They can see it. This is a technological age. When you know what you are doing, when you know it works, when you know it enhances the group work, it creates an ambience of its own. It is very beautiful. It is also a symbol of the efficacy of what one is doing. People say: "Was I doing anything? I don't know. I didn't seem to be concentrating tonight. I didn't feel I was doing much." But if there is an instrument there, somehow they know it is doing the work. If *they* are not doing it, *it* is doing it.

How about the orientation of the tetrahedron? Should the open end face north or south?

You do not have to orient the tetrahedron at all. The magnetic field produced by those magnets is actually more powerful than the earth's magnetic field. If there were no instrumentation in it and it were aligned north-south, it would draw energy from the mental plane. But we are not conditioned by that fact because the energy is not coming from the mental plane of the earth. The energy is coming from Hierarchy. The instrument is bringing it down onto the mental plane by the fact that it is a tetrahedron, because that is the energetic property of that shape — its shape-power. So you do not align it. You can turn it any way you like. What you should not do is to have its gold disk face anyone. The group should be a half-circle, a horseshoe, rather than a full circle. Sometimes, with a lot of people, the circle goes right around the instrument. The Master will say: "We'll bend the beam", but it is better that the group sit on each side so that the beam of blended energies from the gold disk goes out into the world without someone standing in the way of it.

Does our regular Transmission session become an over-shadowing of the group when Benjamin Creme takes part in it?

When I am involved, the transmission of energies becomes an overshadowing by the Christ. I am overshadowed by Him and this becomes a group overshadowing. The Christ nourishes the spiritual life of each person taking part in the Transmission, so that from then on your Transmission work will be heightened.

One of the roles of Maitreya the Christ is to act as the "nourisher of the little ones", "the babes in Christ", that is those who have taken the first and second initiations and need His spiritual "nourishment" to prepare them for the third, the *transfiguration*, which, from the point of view of Hierarchy is only the first true soul initiation.

An experiment is under way, through the agency of a disciple overshadowed by Maitreya, in which this "nourishment" is also given to those who, perhaps, have taken only the *first* initiation. At the same time you are automatically linked to the network of light which Christ is creating in the world. There is a network of light into which you as individual members of each Transmission group and each group as a whole are linked, so that every time you sit down in your group to transmit, you are automatically linked to that group on the inner planes which the Christ nourishes for the work in this coming time. He is always looking for those aspirants and disciples in the world through whom He can work. The Christ has not come to change the world. He has come to show *us* how to change the world. He is here to galvanize us, to inspire us, to guide us, to evoke from us what is already within; but He is not going to do the work. We have got to do it ourselves.

Do the blessings (during Transmission) go on transforming us even if we are asleep?

Yes, the blessings are transforming the person. They emerge from the soul-plane and are given to the souls of the individuals: that is what alignment is about; that is why, during Transmission Meditation, you have to stay aligned. The physical brain has to have the one-pointed and solid connection and alignment with the soul, otherwise that aspect of the communicating channel is missing.

Many people, even if they are not asleep, ruminate; they are in a kind of 'astral daze' for much of the Transmission. That is why the average Transmission time is three-and-a-half minutes rather than 60 minutes per hour. If the alignment were constant the true Transmission time would be 60 minutes in the hour. It is very important, therefore, that you keep that alignment. The person involved receives the blessing; the person is the soul. We are souls, we have to get used to thinking of ourselves as souls — the soul in incarnation is the true man. This personality, with its threefold body, is simply a mechanism, a vehicle, for the true man or woman who is the soul, and it is the soul which receives the blessing. That blessing, of course, has an effect on the vehicles, stimulating the substance of the physical, the astral and the mental bodies, but the actual blessing is for the evolving Son of God in incarnation.

I have heard that touching each other can transfer lower vibrations from one to the other. Why, then, when you preside at a Transmission Meditation, do you ask people to hold hands?

When Benjamin Creme is present, Transmission becomes an overshadowing by the Christ, and the group holds hands.

If it is true that by touching each other we can transfer "lower vibrations" from one to the other, then it must be equally true that by touching each other we can transfer higher vibrations in the same way. During a Transmission Meditation at which I am present, I am overshadowed by Maitreya, Who is Himself overshadowed by the Spirit of Peace and is transmitting the energy of the Avatar of Synthesis (or the Shamballa Force) and that of the Buddha. Through me, and by the group holding hands, this becomes a group overshadowing (the group is spiritually 'nourished' by Maitreya, as I have stated above). In my experience, those people most afraid of 'lower vibrations' — always from other people — leave something to be desired in their own.

(1) Is it necessary for us to hold hands during our regular Transmission sessions when Benjamin Creme is not present? (2) Is it possible for an overshadowing to take place during Transmission through someone else in the group, when Benjamin Creme is not present?

(1) No, it is not necessary to hold hands. (2) When I am not present, an overshadowing does not take place. It is possible for some kind of overshadowing by astral entities to take place through mediumistic people in the group. People with strong mediumistic tendencies could open themselves for use by such entities on the astral plane if their attention drops to the solar plexus during Transmission. Those people have to mentally decide not to be used by astral entities and keep the alignment between the soul and the brain by holding their attention at the ajna centre during Transmission. This is *very important.* One must learn to distinguish between spiritual energies and energies of the astral plane. Transmission Meditation does not deal with astral energies, and, of course, the Masters in charge of the Transmission would not allow interference by astral energy.

Benjamin Creme is regularly overshadowed by Maitreya at the beginning and end of his public lectures. Many people report seeing him surrounded by a brilliant halo of light, while some see him actually 'disappear' in the light. From time to time, the camera, too, registers this phenomenon. This photograph was taken at the beginning of the 1993 Tokyo lecture and shows Benjamin Creme bathed in light, while his interpreter, Michiko Ishikawa, remains in normal light, except for the shoulder nearest Creme.

Are initiations taking place during the overshadowing by Maitreya at your lectures?

In the sense of the major planetary initiations, no; in the sense that every transfer of power is an initiation, then yes. The power released and the stimulus to the force centres (chakras) of the audience which takes place are an initiation of sorts. The individuals in the audience are changed, their vibrational rate heightened, their state of being altered to the degree that they can respond to and absorb the energies.

[*Editor's note*: For more information on initiation, see *Maitreya's Mission,* Vols. I and II, by Benjamin Creme.]

If it is harmful for young children to be in a room where Transmission Meditation is taking place, is it also harmful for them to be present during the overshadowing by Maitreya at the lectures?

No. Since their chakras are still in the process of stabilization, during a Transmission Meditation they would have to be continually shielded by the Masters from the full impact of the energies transmitted. This is a waste of the Masters' energy. At the lectures, however, the Christ can easily regulate the amount of energy which each person receives. I am fully aware of the increase and decrease of the potency for each individual I look at during the overshadowing.

What would you say about the place of cigarettes, alcohol, or drugs like marijuana and LSD? Do these interfere with Transmission?

If they work against the physical body, which they tend to do, they will work against its ability to absorb and stand the impact of the spiritual potencies, which are very great. The purer the body, the easier it is to absorb these potencies. But one must not be fanatical about it. I am not a guru and I am not telling you what to do, but I would see as a precondition for Transmission work the giving up of anything to do with drugs. Drugs are very much contra-indicative to any kind of spiritual path because they ruin the nervous system. The nervous system is the link on the physical plane between the soul and its vehicle. On the etheric levels there is a correspondence to the physical nervous system. It is composed of countless light fibers called "nadis" which underlie the entire nervous system. When death occurs, the etheric body loosens itself from the dense physical body through the snapping away of the nadis from the nervous system.

LSD or any of the hallucinatory drugs have a deleterious effect on the nervous system. Some of the effects are known and some are quite unknown. There is always a danger of damaging the web of nadis between the physical and etheric planes. Much of the hallucinatory experience of those on drugs is due to this destruction, and it can lead to insanity.

Do you consider pot (marijuana) a drug?

Oh, yes, very much so. It has a long-term deleterious effect on the nervous system. If you meditate, you should not take pot.

Tobacco?

Tobacco is unpleasant and also lowers the vitality of the body and I would recommend that it be completely avoided.

What about alcohol?

Alcohol has two kinds of influence. A small amount of alcohol has a positive effect on the body. It is a stimulating tonic. A large amount of alcohol has a deleterious effect and should be avoided.

And aspirin?

Aspirin is a poison. It should be totally eschewed. I recommend, if you want an ameliorative drug, that you take only homeopathic potencies which are so refined as to be almost totally harmless. Instead of taking aspirin for a headache you could take aconite.

Is there anything we can do in our lives such as changing our diet that would increase the purity of our physical bodies?

Yes, but I am not the one to answer these questions, because I am not that disciplined. I forget about the physical body. I seldom think about it. I eat what I like, drink what I like and leave my physical body to get on and do what it has to do. I do not eat meat and I avoid what I know makes me ill. You can eat as much meat as you like and still do Transmission, but if you want to take initiation, if you want to make fast spiritual progress, if you want to absorb as much of the spiritual energies at as high a rate as possible (as high as your body will take), then you should not eat meat. Fish is neutral. Poultry is preferable to meat but it is not totally neutral as is fish. Vegetarianism should be the norm for a disciple. But it is better not to be fanatical about diet. The body is not that important except for those approaching the first initiation. After that, dietary discipline (with common sense and sense of proportion) should be automatic.

As the mind tends to become rather lulled while one is digesting a meal, eating prior to meditation is not recommended. (1) Would this be the case in relation to taking part in Transmission Meditation? (2) If so, how long prior to sitting ought one to have completed a meal? Or does it not matter at all?

(1) Yes; too heavy a meal dulls the awareness and mental focus necessary in Transmission Meditation. (2) Each person digests at a different speed so definite figures are not possible. I would suggest at least an hour's interval before the Transmission as reasonable and a light meal as desirable.

[*Editor's note*: In-depth discussions on how to maintain the alignment between the soul and the physical brain, essential for an effective Transmission, are printed in Chapter IX, "Maintaining Alignment".]

CHAPTER VI

THE NATURE OF TRANSMISSION

Where do the energies come from for Transmission Meditation and what kinds of energies are they?

The subject of Transmission from the point of view of the Masters is so complex, so esoteric, that I could not really begin to tell you what it is from Their point of view. I have asked this question of my own Master and He has said to me: "There is no way I could explain. You would never understand." This difficulty arises because we do not know the techniques or instruments They use. But suffice it to say that They receive energy from many different sources: Shamballa energy from Shamballa, the head centre of the planet; extra-systemic energy from the other planets and the sun itself; and extra-solar energy from Sirius and the Great Bear, the origin of the seven rays.

The Masters Themselves form a Hierarchy. The Christ is the Master of all the Masters and is the recipient par excellence within the Hierarchy for the various energies. In fact, today He is almost entirely in charge of the distribution of these energies. All of the Masters are engaged in transmitting energy, but the Christ decides precisely which energies, and in what balance, will be distributed at any given time. He Himself, as anyone who has studied the Alice Bailey teachings will know, is the recipient today of very specific energies which He transmits into the world.

He receives energy from an Avatar called the Avatar of Synthesis, a great Being from outside this solar system who was invoked during the 1940s by the Hierarchy. This Avatar brings in all three of the divine aspects, or divine energies that we recognize — the Will, Love, and Intelligence aspects, together with another aspect for which we do not as yet have a name. That fourfold energy, very similar to the Shamballa or Will energy, is distributed into the world by the Christ. It brings about synthesis in the world. The effect of this energy as it plays upon humanity is to bring humanity together.

The energy of Synthesis works only through groups, not through individuals. It works through Hierarchy as a group and through humanity itself as a group. It works through the United Nations General Assembly (but not the Security Council). It works through the major and most important group in the world, the New Group of World Servers, which was formed by the Christ in 1922. This group has a close relationship, subjectively, with Hierarchy. On the outer plane it is divided into two groups: a large outer group unaware of their subjective relation to Hierarchy, who work under impression from the Masters; and a small inner nucleus who work quite consciously under the supervision of the Masters. The members of that group are distributed throughout the world, in every country without exception, men and women in all walks of life. They are the most important group in the world today. They are a subjective group without any outer organization. The Avatar of Synthesis works through all groups, bringing humanity together, synthesizing it into the unity which it essentially is.

The second energy which the Christ distributes in this way is that of the Spirit of Peace or Equilibrium. This is a great Cosmic Being embodying the energy of love at a cosmic level. He overshadows the Christ, Maitreya, in a way similar to the Christ's overshadowing of the Master Jesus in Palestine. He works very closely with the Law of Action and Reaction. The effect of His work in the world is to transform and transmute the prevalent hatred, violence, and discord into their exact opposites, so that we shall enter an era of peace, tranquility, and emotional and mental poise, balanced in exact proportion to the present chaos. That is the effect of the energy of this great Avatar of Peace.

The third source of Divine energy is the Buddha, the Brother of the Christ, Who brings in the Wisdom energy. The Christ is the Embodiment of Love. The Buddha is the Embodiment of

Wisdom. They work together all the time, daily, hourly. They even share a level of consciousness. The Buddha has taken a great Cosmic Initiation in recent years, which allows Him to bring in the Wisdom energy from cosmic levels. He transmits it to the Christ and the Christ transmits it into the world. The Christ thus stands as the point within a triangle of force from the Avatar of Synthesis, the Spirit of Peace, and the Buddha, and transmits Their energies into the world.

The energies are sent by the Christ through one or two Masters and then through the Transmission groups. They step them down to a potency humanity can absorb. If the Transmission group has the tetrahedron instrument, that device steps them down even further. In the field of electricity, transformers are used to lower voltage and make a voltage, which might otherwise harm you, usable and safe. In the same way, the Transmission groups act as transformers. The energies are stepped down and transformed. Of course they lose potency after being stepped down, but become usable and transformative in the world.

Can you say something about the True Spirit of the Christ?

One of the energies which flows from Maitreya during Transmission Meditation is the True Spirit of the Christ. This is the Christ Principle, the Christ Consciousness, the energy which He uniquely embodies in the world. That makes Him the Christ. The Christ is the man Who embodies the Christ Principle. This energy flows from Him in enormous potency. During a Transmission, it flows with the other energies, but from time to time He releases it apart from the other energies.

What is the difference between the overshadowing of Maitreya during Transmission Meditation, the Christ Principle, and the phase during Transmission when you say: "This is the true Spirit of the Christ"?

When I say: "This is the true Spirit of the Christ", it is to let you know that during the phase that follows Maitreya is releasing specifically what we call the Christ Principle, the energy of consciousness itself. That is the energy He embodies. We call it love, and it flows very potently during that phase. It flows at other times during the Transmission, perhaps most of the time, but because it is mixed in with other energies you do not recognize it. During that phase, He releases it purely. That is why for many people this is the most magical, wonderful part of a Transmission. They feel that wonderful energy of love; they are bathed in it. It is powerful, magnetic. You can bathe in it, feel it all around you; you are floating in a sea of love, which it is. It is a wonderful experience. That is the energy of consciousness.

On the Day of Declaration, that energy will pour out in tremendous potency through the hearts of everybody in the world. Maitreya has said: "It will be as if I embrace the whole world. People will feel it even physically." That is why we say: "Love makes the world go round."

Love literally makes the world go around because it is the energy of evolution. Without that energy, there would be no evolution. There would not be the longing, the aspiration, the aiming higher, to what? Why does humanity know that it evolves? Why does humanity aspire to what we call betterment? Why do we do it? Not because churches tell us, but because our soul tells us — as soon as we make any degree of conscious contact with the soul.

What does Hierarchy do with all these energies?

Only Hierarchy knows that. They send them where they are needed, which might be to a particular country or area in the world, or else simply to top up, or keep at a high level, the reservoir of spiritual energies in the world. It is very important indeed that people in Transmission groups do not direct the energies. They should leave this to the Masters, who alone know where they are needed and in what particular balance and potency. This is a moment-to-moment changing situation that only the Christ has the science to understand. So, although you might think: "What a good idea to send some good energy to the Middle East", you could be doing entirely the wrong thing. The energy being transmitted through the group at that particular time might be just the energy which is *not* needed in the Middle East. So one should send it to no group, no country, no person in particular.

The Christ is in charge of these energies all the time, from moment to moment. As he looks at the world with all its problems, He thinks about it energetically: That needs stimulus, that needs careful handling, that needs, perhaps, energy withdrawn. Not only that, but all the energies have different qualities. So He does not send one thing we call energy, but the energy of Will, or of Love, or of Organization, or whatever. It is the blending of these which creates the effect in the world. So you can see how useless it is to try to decide for yourself what that energy could or should do. It is such a complex and occult science that only the Masters can know.

How do you know as an individual that you are not contacting energy which would be dangerous to yourself?

You do not know; humanity has not yet the science whereby it can judge the value or the danger of any particular energy. These energies impinge on this planet from the cosmos and there is nothing humanity at its present stage can do about it. Hence the continuing need for the Hierarchy of Masters standing behind the world.

They are the inner government of the planet. They are the custodians of all the energies pouring into the earth. In Their hands lies its destiny. They are major scientists who respond to and know the value and danger of any particular energy impinging on this planet. They manipulate the energies scientifically, offsetting some, protecting us from the impact of others, and channelling those which we need and can use.

In this coming Age of Aquarius we ourselves shall become the custodians of these energies, with the Hierarchy of Masters living among us once again, teaching and guiding us. We will learn to utilize, channel, and manipulate the energies of the universe, energies of which today we are totally unaware. Some of them are highly dangerous indeed; some of them are of the greatest benefit. But even the most beneficial energy is of little value to humanity if it is at a potency higher than our centres can stand; hence the need for protection. The Masters act as a protective grid, as do certain great devas or angels, to shield humanity from these potentially harmful energies; there need be no fear about this. There is no way we can tell if we are contacting them, but the Masters take care of them for us.

When we sit in Transmission groups, are we giving or receiving energy?

What we are doing is a service, giving our vehicles as instruments through which the energy can flow. We are not giving energy to anybody; we are receiving it from the Kingdom of Souls, the Spiritual Kingdom, made up of the Masters and the Initiates of the Wisdom. We are receiving it in the sense that it is flowing through us, but it cannot flow through us without stimulating the centres through which it moves, and we also receive benefits from transmitting this energy.

Through which chakras do the energies come in, and through which do they go out?

This depends on the individual's point of evolution and therefore which chakras are open and can be used. With the majority, the heart, throat, and ajna are used. With some, the crown chakra is also utilized. With some, more advanced, all seven chakras are used.

90

It also depends on the ray structure of the person involved, the line of force on which people are, as souls, as personalities, with mental, astral, and physical bodies — all of these may be on different rays. So it is not possible to say these energies come through one centre and go out through another, because it depends on the individual. People vary enormously in the state of development of the individual chakras. If a chakra through which that particular ray-energy would normally flow is not open enough, other chakras can be used by the Masters to transmit. There is a limit to the extent to which this can be done, but within these limits it is done.

Broadly speaking, people will receive and transmit energies along their own line of force. There are seven lines of force, seven ray-energies, and people can be along the 2-4-6 line, or the 1-3-5-7 line. A group may be made up of people of all different rays. While the energies are being transmitted you might find that half the group is transmitting the 2-4-6 ray energies and the other half transmitting the 1-3-5-7 ray energies. There are also some groups which are on one line or the other. But there is a movement in the Hierarchy whereby the disciples are being given the opportunity, more and more, to handle the energies of the line which is not their own.

Is there a connection between Transmission Meditation and kundalini?

Transmission Meditation necessarily involves the awakening and correct directing of the kundalini energy locked at the base of the spine. The base chakra is always the last to be activated, the kundalini being then gradually raised through the already prepared higher centres in a special sequence, depending on the individual. This scientific process is in the expert hands of the Masters directing the Transmission. There is nothing anyone need 'do' about it. Premature awakening and raising of the kundalini, without preparation of the higher chakras, is highly dangerous and should not be attempted.

(1) If kundalini rises is this an initiation or enlightenment? (2) Are you changed after this has happened?

It depends on the situation. Many people practise some form of kundalini-yoga and deliberately arouse the kundalini energy, dormant at the base of the spine. This is extremely dangerous unless done under the supervision of an advanced initiate teacher. The fact that the fire of kundalini can be so roused does not constitute either initiation or enlightenment. It could lead to madness if the chakras are not prepared in advance to receive it. In the normal course of life, kundalini is rising all the time, but in small, controlled amounts, thus safely. The regulated life of service is the best guarantee of safe kundalini control. When it is scientifically guided through the chakras, prepared in the correct sequence, there will eventuate a degree of enlightenment and, if the person is ready, initiation.

Does the individual experience positive effects when transmitting energy?

The Christ and the Masters now have at their disposal cosmic energies which They have never had before, in a potency altogether new. Transmission work is a very dynamic process of sending these energies to the world. You cannot do it without receiving them through your centres, which are charged, activated and heightened in their activity as a result.

When the Masters measure advancement, they look clairvoyantly into the world. They do not look into your thoughts to see if you are thinking good or bad thoughts — not at all. They see an individual's inner light, a dim light or a bright one. When They see a steady, brilliant light, They take interest in that individual. They look at the state of the centres to assess his or her exact point in evolution. They can tell at a glance which centres are open or activated, how much they are open, whether they are spinning fast or slowly and in which direction, the colours they emit, the quality of the aura, and so on. They can then evaluate the individual accordingly.

In Transmission Meditation, the Masters choose the amount of energy for a particular person and They send it through you. You can understand how potent the transmission of energy from Them can be. I do not know of anything which is more potent from the personal, evolutionary viewpoint.

It is a hothouse, a forcing process. In a year of this Transmission work, you can make the inner growth resulting from many years of other forms of meditation. There are a great many meditations and yoga techniques which aim at the same stimulation of the centres and, while they may have value and relevance, they can be dangerous unless they are done under the guidance of a Master. Transmission work, on the other hand, is always done under the supervision of the Masters and is perfectly safe.

As you continue to do Transmission work, does your environment change as you do, does it evolve as you evolve?

Necessarily so, because you become more radiatory. You radiate a higher frequency of energy and therefore have more impact on your environment. That impact can be for either good or ill, depending on the motive. If you are taking part in Transmission work of this kind, your motive will be one of service to the world and will inevitably have a beneficial effect on your environment. That is not to say that your environment will necessarily respond to it in a positive way, because it will produce change. Every inflow of higher, spiritual energy produces change in the recipient. That is how evolution proceeds: by the nourishment from the kingdom above of the energy which produces the mutation, which produces evolution itself. So those with whom you live and work will certainly notice a change in your make-up. Those who enter meditation sometimes change profoundly, depending on their character and on the depth to which the soul has penetrated into the individual. You will notice, too, a build-up of energy in the room and house in which the Transmission takes place.

Is Transmission Meditation accelerated on the energetic points of the world, for example, at Stonehenge in England?

No. I believe there is a misapprehension here. The energies transmitted are not dependent on some outer physical stimulus, but on the Plan of the Masters who send them, and on the point of evolution of the people in the transmitting groups. The more evolved the people, the more potent can be the energy safely sent by Hierarchy.

What is the difference between Transmission energies and healing energies?

Healing energies are, for the most part, etheric. They come from the etheric plane, but there is also some soul energy involved. Transmission groups deal with spiritual energies, cosmic in origin, coming from several very high sources as described earlier. It is a different thing from groups sending healing energy to other groups or individuals. Then they would direct it. But as a Transmission group in the terms in which I am speaking, they should not direct the energy. Nor should they see this Transmission Meditation as a way of contacting their 'guides', those on the astral planes whom they believe to be giving them messages.

Some of us who have been working in a Transmission group would like to send 'healing thoughts' to people in need after the Transmission ends. Would you please recommend some hints, guidelines, or methods which are in line with this?

A simple and effective technique is the following: holding the mind "steady in the light" (focused in the ajna centre), visualize and/or name the people one after the other. At the same time ask aloud that the healing power of God be directed to those in need. This invocation will find response in certain Masters Who, either directly or through Their disciples, will carry out the healing (within, of course, the limits of karma).

Could you please explain what is meant by "holding the mind steady in the light"?

Through meditation correctly carried out, the antahkarana, or channel of light between the physical brain and the soul, is gradually built and strengthened. By means of that channel, the soul light is anchored in the head of the disciple. This is seen as a brilliant light within the head during meditation. With the attention drawn inward and upward in that light, the mind is held "steady", that is, without thought or movement of the lower mind. In that condition of thoughtless focused attention, the intuitive levels of the mind can come into play; gradually this becomes an instinctive, fixed condition, needing no formal meditational 'going within' to bring about.

Many people believe that any thought or idea that enters the mind during meditation comes from the intuitional soul level and is guiding their actions. This is by no means the case. It is extremely difficult for the average aspirant or disciple to "hold the mind steady in the light" for long enough to invoke the intuition, and the 'guidance' which most people receive is that of their own lower minds via the subconscious.

Can you explain the building of the antahkarana, the bridge of light?

The construction of the antahkarana, the bridge linking the physical brain with the soul, proceeds according to the effectiveness (more or less scientific) of the person's meditation. Meditation brings about the at-one-ment, through the bridge, of the soul and personality. Eventually three fires or streams of energy are put down by the soul and constitute the channel of communication between soul and brain. Through that channel, the Light, Love, and eventually Will of the soul can make their appearance on the physical plane. The building of the

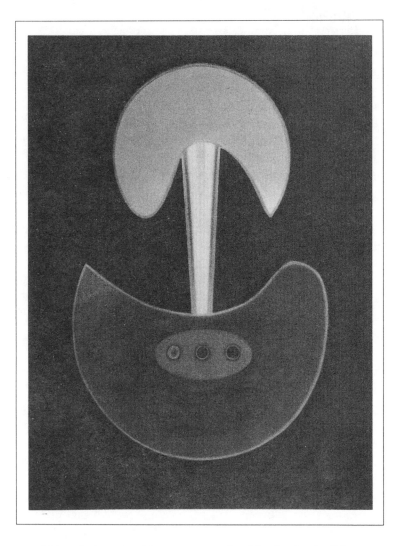

This painting, *Antahkarana*, was painted by Benjamin Creme in 1968. The antahkarana represents the channel or bridge of light which is formed between the personality and the soul through meditation.

antahkarana proceeds unconsciously from the soul down during meditation, and takes several lives to perfect.

Some meditation practices claim not only to help build the antahkarana (channel between the soul and brain) but also, in more advanced forms, to clear away external thoughtforms from the individual's field. Will Transmission Meditation accomplish not only the 'building' of the channel but also the removal of thoughtforms?

No serious — that is, scientific — meditation is designed to "remove thoughtforms". Thoughtforms are the result of the natural God-given capacity of the human mind to think, to create thoughtforms, from which all action stems. The problem lies in the creative or destructive quality of the thoughtforms. Through scientific meditation (and no meditation is more scientific than Transmission Meditation, because it is in the hands of the Master scientists), the antahkarana is created and strengthened, thus allowing the energies of the soul to enter the personality vehicles. These include the energies of the higher mind and Buddhi, which we call the intuition. The thoughtforms stemming from those levels are the creative inspirations of all great achievement and are not ones to be "cleared away from the individual's field".

The thoughtforms which *do* need to be removed are those arising from astral/emotional reactions. These are persistent thought-patterns of a negative nature, which inhibit the downflow and right use of soul energy. These can be removed permanently only by a gradual shift of polarization to the mental plane, thus starving the emotional reactions of their astral nourishment. Meditation of any kind will further this process; Transmission Meditation most certainly will do so because of its unusual potency and scientific basis.

Are there any major differences between the Triangles work and the Transmission Meditation groups which you seek to set up?

Not in principle, but the Transmission group work is more potent and lasts longer. It has other purposes, too. The Triangles movement was inaugurated by the Master Djwhal Khul through Alice Bailey for use with the two earlier parts of the Great Invocation which were released to the world in 1936 and 1940. It was an attempt (and a very successful one) to link people in mental substance — getting them to form a more powerful unit than their own separated selves. The Triangles movement consists in organizing those triangles.

To be a member of a triangle, you simply agree with two friends to form one. You do not have to be in the same location. You do not have to say the Great Invocation at the same time of day. You each say it aloud wherever and whenever it is convenient, and as you do, each of you mentally links up with the two other members of the triangle. Visualize circulating above the heads of the three of you a triangle of white light. See your triangle linked to a network of such triangles which covers the whole world. By saying the Great Invocation you automatically invoke the energy, which is potentized by that triangle in thought, just as it is potentized by the group which is meeting on the physical plane. But meeting on the physical plane adds a dimension, a vitality, which is absent when it is only on the mental plane. It is possible for triangles to act in a linked way and still remain triangles. You can be in a triangle with two people and also in a triangle with two other people, and they in turn each in a triangle with two other people, and so on. So you are part of a network, but you still work in triangular formation. That is the important thing.

But it is even better if you can work together as a Transmission group, quite apart from the triangles which you may have with people with whom you never meet. It is not either/or, but both. More energy from Hierarchy can safely be put through a Transmission group than through the same number of separate individuals. When the individuals are physically present together, energies can be sent at higher potencies and can be circulated among them, creating unique patterns such as triangles, stars, and other configurations. Because the energies are sent in this way, they are specially potentized. There is no real difference between the Triangles work and Transmission groups; the only difference is one of potency and the amount of time devoted to the activity.

Would you say that Transmission Meditation is more potent than any other kind of group meditation?

Yes. Other forms of group meditation depend on the contact of the group with its soul, whereas Transmission Meditation does not. In Transmission, the meditation takes place from the soul level, but it is under the control of the Masters, not of the group. Sitting in group (soul) meditation is useful but in no way as potent and useful as participating in a Transmission group, because then the energy is coming from Hierarchy. In one year of Transmission work, you can make the advance as an individual or as a group that would take many years of ordinary personal or group meditation, however potent that might be. Of course, the more developed the individuals, the more soul-infused the group, the more potent the Transmission Meditation. But whatever level we happen to be at, our work and our service activity are potentized more by Transmission Meditation than by any other form. That is why it is given at this time.

If one is in a Transmission group, is it all right to take part in other types of group meditation or study with a particular guru?

Yes. Transmission Meditation does not work against any other form of meditation. Indeed, it will enhance the quality and effectiveness of any other meditation you may do. Every individual today, whatever his level, his background, his type of mind, and tradition has a teaching, a path, a meditation, or a guru available to him. All true gurus are members of the Hierarchy at some level, initiates of some degree. The more developed the individual, the higher the guru he will be attracted to.

These gurus are themselves centres of force who act as transmitters of energy from their Masters. Usually gurus are from the Indian tradition in which there is a direct lineage from guru to guru to devotee. But within the Hierarchy it is done in a less individualistic way. It is not usually transmitted through one point, although it may be. There may be one person in a Transmission group who acts as the nucleus of that group and through whom the energy flows more directly and more potently, and in this way, without being a guru in any kind of educative sense, he or she acts as a point of greater force within the group.

I was introduced to Transmission Meditation recently by someone who belonged to a certain group, and I began to take part in it because I was attracted by the idea of world service. However, I do not feel comfortable about taking part in the group's other activity. Will it be necessary for me to do both if I want to continue Transmission Meditation work?

No. There are groups using Transmission Meditation who are also involved in various activities such as psychic development, teachings through mediums, other forms of meditation using various techniques, study groups, etc. They are mostly self-oriented, self-centred types of activities. I would like to make it very clear that there is no connection between the two activities. Transmission Meditation is a purely scientific form in which the Masters of Hierarchy send spiritual energies into the world through Transmission Meditation groups, and is undertaken with altruistic motivation to serve the world. It should not be confused with any other type of activity.

In response to my Master's request, we have not created any walls (such as naming the group, organization, officers, secretaries, etc.) around Transmission Meditation work, and any individual or any group with aspiration to co-operate with Hierarchy can take up this work. While doing Transmission Meditation, inevitably the spiritual growth of the individual or the group will be accelerated and their other activities will become more potent.

However, the two should never be confused. The people who join to do Transmission Meditation should not be pressured into taking part in the group's other activities, and vice versa. A certain time should be put aside just to do Transmission Meditation.

Please tell me what is meant by the phrases 'Transmission Meditation' and 'Transcendental Meditation'. Which of the two should a comparative beginner adopt and for how long should the meditation be sustained?

Transcendental Meditation is a form of meditation introduced to the West by Maharishi Mahesh Yogi many years ago and it has adherents, I would think, in most countries of the world. It is a form of personal meditation which can be expanded into group meditation. There are, as it were, higher and higher courses to take.

Transmission Meditation on the other hand was introduced through me by my Master. It provides an opportunity for *service* for those taking part in transmitting spiritual energies from the Hierarchy of Masters, thus stepping them down and making them more accessible. This is done in groups and is a very potent form of service on the one hand and personal growth on the other.

It is not a question of doing one form of meditation or the other. I would certainly recommend that everyone who wishes to take up Transmission Meditation. I know of nothing of more value to the individual or the planet. But its practice does not rule out any form of personal meditation which attracts the individual. Transcendental Meditation is a very simple method which most people can do, and I would certainly recommend it to anyone. The beginner is, I believe, normally advised to meditate for 15 to 20 minutes twice a day, and for personal meditation this is adequate. Transmission Meditation on the other hand can go on for a very long time.

Do TM (Transcendental Meditation) and Zen meditation groups transmit without knowing it?

Not in the manner of the Transmission groups who invoke and transmit the energies of Hierarchy. In TM and Zen meditation (and all personal meditation), the energy is received from the meditator's own soul, but sometimes also from a Master, for instance, from Guru Dev for people in TM. In order for the Hierarchy to use a group for the transmission of energy, there has to be a conscious willingness on the part of the meditators to co-operate with the Christ and the Masters. They will never infringe upon our free will. If the Great Invocation is used, it will be a Transmission.

You have said that Transmission Meditation is compatible with TM (Transcendental Meditation). Does this go for Kriya Yoga?

Yes. Transmission Meditation is compatible with all other forms of meditation and can only enhance the effect of any others used. It is, in fact, a form of Kriya Yoga, but the work is done for one by the Masters, totally scientifically and occultly correct. Kriya Yoga is a powerful yoga of the centres in which one mentally guides the energy around the chakras over and over again. It is very strenuous and takes a great deal of concentration and effort. Something similar takes place in Transmission Meditation, but it is done by the Masters more scientifically than anybody could do by himself or herself.

There are many different meditation techniques available today; some systems, such as Transcendental Meditation or Zen do not stress the need for any moral qualifications before meditating. Others state that meditation, without the basis of a 'good character', is dangerous. Can Transcendental Meditation or any form of meditation be undertaken when there are aspects of one's nature still uncontrolled?

All meditation is 'dangerous' in that it upsets the 'status quo'. The effect on the lower bodies of the soul energy invoked by meditation is always disturbing (at first) to the 'lower man'. This need not cause major concern in most cases, as equilibrium (at a higher vibration) is usually re-established before long. This process of disturbance and re-establishing of equilibrium is repeated over and over again until the third initiation can be taken. 'Good character' should not be equated with total control of the lower, personality nature. If total control were required to begin meditation, no one except the highest initiates could start. The important requirement (and safeguard) is that the soul energy invoked by meditation should be utilized in some form of altruistic service. Otherwise, all sorts of difficulties, illnesses and/or neuroses can result.

Is it true that meditation lowers the crime rate as TM meditators maintain?

I believe it does to some extent. All human action is the result of the response to energies and the ideas embodying energies. A large group of people engaged in dynamic meditation set up thought waves of a constructive kind which must have some influence on the surrounding mental atmosphere.

Can Transmission Meditation be practised daily as a form of personal meditation or must it be practised only in a group at an appointed time?

Transmission Meditation is essentially a group meditation and a form of group service. It can, of course, be practised together with a personal meditation and will enhance the effect of the latter.

What is the relationship between personal meditation and Transmission Meditation? Is personal meditation essential for making progress?

Transmission Meditation will enhance the personal meditation and the personal meditation will reinforce the efficiency of your Transmission Meditation.

Personal meditation is not essential for making progress, but it is very useful. It is one way, among others, to make progress.

In a meditation group, if some people are attempting a Transmission Meditation while others are performing a personal meditation not based on Transmission and service, is any transmission of energy limited to those members consciously performing Transmission Meditation, or does everyone contribute?

The transmission of energies from Hierarchy would be limited to those doing Transmission Meditation. Those doing a personal meditation might well receive the energy of their own souls.

Is not any gathering for prayer or meditation a form of transmission?

If invocation is involved — prayer is a form of astral invocation — then yes. But simple personal meditation, whether individually or in groups, does not necessarily involve transmission beyond the participants.

Can you describe the differences between prayer, meditation, and Transmission?

Prayer is an expression of supplication usually manifested through the solar plexus; it may also, at its highest, contain energies of the heart, as an unspoken communion, heart-to-heart, with the Divine Source of which we are a part.

The solar plexus is the seat of the emotions, of the astral nature ("astral" and "emotional" are synonymous terms), and the heart is the seat of the higher astral and the spiritual aspiration. The aim of the evolutionary process humanity is going through is to shift from the almost totally emotional response, which is prevalent in the world, to the heart response, thus changing emotion into love.

The astral body, the body of the emotions, was evolved in humanity during the Atlantean race. This was a long period of time, from 12 million to about 98,000 years ago. During that racial experience humanity perfected the astral body — its sensory, feeling, emotional body. So well did Atlantean man perform that task that the astral body is the most powerful vehicle that humanity has today.

Most of us are emotionally polarized and are swept by the energies of the astral plane. They cause havoc in humanity and are the source of most of our problems and difficulties. The sooner humanity can use the mental plane to control the energies of the astral plane and lift them up to the heart centre, the sooner humanity will begin its progress into divinity.

In fact, the Master D.K. has said that the most important thing you can do, the greatest gift you can give to the world, the greatest service you can perform, is to control your astral vehicle. As soon as you control that vehicle, that which was astral energy becomes transmuted into love. The activity of the solar plexus is then relegated to that of absorbing energy from the sun, which galvanizes the physical body. Through the spleen that energy is distributed throughout the body as a whole, while the emotional energy is lifted up and expressed through the heart as love. The astral body is meant to be like a mirror — a still pool in which the Buddhic level, the spiritual intuition, can be reflected. For most people it is a churning cauldron, swept willy-nilly by all the emotions to which we are prone. Until we conquer these and transmute them into love, we cannot become divine. But when we do, we take the first step into divinity.

Prayer at its best is aspiration. The higher the aspiration, the more heart activity it will involve. Meditation is the means par excellence of becoming aligned with, and gradually infused by, the energy of the soul, the Higher Self. It is the mode of bringing us into at-one-ment with the soul. Invocation is something different, and Transmission is allied to invocation. It is the calling out of energy from a higher spiritual source and the transmission of that energy to a lower source. Transmission is a bridge between the higher source, Hierarchy, and the lower source, humanity in general.

What is the difference between the energies transmitted through Transmission groups and those utilized, for instance, in the rituals of the Liberal Catholic Church or other temple services?

The difference is not great except in the method used. The transmission of energies is the same, however it occurs. The people engaged in these exoteric religious observances may have no idea that they are transmitting energy. Yet when you go into any of the great cathedrals of the world, if you are sensitive to energy at all you will become aware of the sometimes tremendous vibration in these buildings. They are usually built on power centres. They are energized and potentized by the Christ and the Masters and are meant to be centres of force and healing, although they are seldom, if ever, used as such by the Christian groups. In other parts of the world, in temples and other power centres, the energies are used therapeutically as they were intended.

In the Liberal Catholic Church, the transmission of energy is done much more consciously and deliberately. The participants experience the energy more directly. The invocation is the actual ritual of the ceremony. Transmission is much simpler, more scientific, and without ritual.

When a group is transmitting, what is to prevent some entity or entities from directing the energies where they wish? Isn't it a glamour to think the Masters are directing the energies? Aren't you in a sense relinquishing your free will?

If you are working in a Transmission group, it can be assumed, I think, that you will have accepted that the energies being channelled through you come from Hierarchy. Since this is the case, is it not also logical that the Masters send these energies consciously, scientifically, directing them according to potency, balance, and destination? This being so, is it not also logical to assume that being Master Scientists and Knowers, They can and do prevent any interference with Their purposes and work? Transmission Meditation is an act of service, willingly undertaken. In no sense, therefore, is one relinquishing one's free will.

In our private Transmission Meditation, are Sai Baba, the Avatar of Synthesis, and the Spirit of Peace automatically invoked through the use of the Great Invocation/Messages from Maitreya, as in the group overshadowing which takes place at your public lectures/Transmission workshops?

No. I am afraid there are misunderstandings in this question. Sai Baba is not "invoked" at public meetings — nor are the Avatar of Synthesis and the Spirit of Peace. The presence of the energies of the Avatar of Synthesis, the Spirit of Peace, and the Buddha are the result of the overshadowing of myself by Maitreya; through me this becomes a group overshadowing. The overshadowing of myself by Sai Baba, when it occurs, — usually in response to my answering a question about him — is at his whim or decision.

To what degree is the transmission of energies actually working?

It is not possible for us to know exactly how effective is the transmission of energies, but the fact that Hierarchy *sends* the energies and encourages the formation of Transmission groups shows the importance that They place on this work. My information is that it is without doubt of primary importance.

(1) In what way are 24-hour Transmissions different from ordinary, regular Transmissions? (2) Is it not better to really concentrate and transmit well for, say 10 hours/five hours/three

hours with 10 or 20 people than 24 hours with, at times, only three people?

(1) They are much longer! Also, they are infrequent, perhaps three times, only, a year, at the major Spring Festivals of Easter, Wesak and of Humanity. (2) The answer here is a qualified yes. The Three Spring Festivals, however, provide a unique opportunity for groups around the world to establish together a potent rhythm. Throughout 24 hours, Hierarchy can link all working groups together into the global network of light which They are constantly creating and potentizing. There is also a powerful psychological factor involved, namely the added stimulus to aspiration and service which the celebration of these Festivals promotes.

At Easter we had a 15-hour Transmission Meditation with our group. As the group is not so large, there were hardly more than three people at a time transmitting in rota. Is it not better, therefore, to have a shorter Transmission with, for example, eight or 10 people at a time?

Not necessarily. It depends on the circumstances. Certainly at the major Festivals a long Transmission is valuable even if few are engaged at any given time.

(1) Is full-moon meditation as important as Transmission Meditation? (2) Will it become a special celebration?

(1) Yes. (2) Yes.

Is Transmission work particularly important now while we wait for the emergence of the Christ? Will it be just as valuable after the emergence?

It is impossible to overemphasize the importance of the work of Transmission groups. This is probably the most important work that all of us can easily be engaged in, whatever other activities we might have in connection with the Plan or whatever other service activity we might be involved in. At present it is of vital importance in creating a pool of energy and, in conjunction with meditation and prayer, helping to invoke the Christ into the outer arena of the world, to enable Him to begin His mission in the full open sense of the word.

Transmission work will most certainly be useful after the official appearance of the Christ and the Masters. In fact it is a continuous activity into the New Age and beyond. The Masters in Their own high way are transmitting energies from higher sources 24 hours a day. It is the major work of Hierarchy and knows no end.

You claim that Transmission Meditation is so extraordinary that, over and above its value as a field of service, its "secondary" effects are so powerful for those who practise it as to accelerate their development perhaps 10 times faster than any other form of personal meditation. (1) How is it that you are alone in presenting this form of meditation? (2) Why do great spiritual beings like Sai Baba, Premananda and others not recommend it? (3) Why is it that even Maitreya, in the Messages given through you, does not speak about it?

(1) Transmission Meditation is a Hierarchical endeavour, presented to disciples and aspirants as a potent field of service by my Master, through me. Its presentation is part, therefore, of my *own* service activity. (2) That it is not expressly recommended by Sai Baba or Swami Premananda is beside the point — They do not recommend people to read Krishnamurti, practise Kriya Yoga, or read Alice Bailey. That is not Their task. As a matter of fact, Transmission Meditation is the only meditation (other than His own) allowed by Sai Baba to be practised in His ashram. (3) Nowhere, in the 140 Messages given publicly through me, does Maitreya mention meditation at all. It is not His major concern.

Should Transmission Meditation be taught in schools? If so, at what age?

No, Transmission Meditation, to my mind, cannot be seen as a general school subject. It is a form of service which, by its very nature, attracts only disciples wishing to serve. No child under the age of 12, in any case, should do Transmission Meditation.

CHAPTER VII

HIGHER AND LOWER PSYCHISM

How does the energy from the Masters differ from psychic energy?

It depends on what you mean by "psychic energy". The psychic utilizes energy at many different levels; there is lower psychism and higher psychism. Higher psychism uses spiritual energies, while lower psychism uses astral energy. The Masters themselves use only higher psychism — higher telepathy, higher clairvoyance, higher clairaudience, using the centres in the soul through the physical brain. Lower psychism works through the solar plexus centre and has to do only with the astral plane, which the Masters are not interested in at all. They transmit Their energies through the higher centres: the heart, the throat and the head centres. In the longer term this will stimulate higher psychic activity, but not the lower psychic activity of the astral nature.

Is a spirit guide the same thing as a Master?

No. I have used the term "guide" for a Master; the Masters are the guides, the guardians, the protectors, the inspirers of our race, our culture, our civilization. But there are many spiritualist groups gathered around a medium who has a spirit guide or guides. These guides are not Masters. The Masters never use that form of lower psychism. The Masters can be contacted only on the higher mental planes. They do not use the astral planes, which the vast majority of the mediums of the world contact during their seances. These "guides" are disciples, if they are at all evolved, but very often they are no more evolved than the people through whom they are speaking. They can be mischievous or beneficent entities on the astral plane or, if the medium is evolved enough, certain discarnate beings who make it their work to help and give aspirational guidance from the higher astral planes. It depends on the evolution of the medium, the quality of the group around him or her, and the ability of the medium to contact a high enough level of the astral or the lower mental planes.

How can we distinguish higher level guidance?

You will know by the quality of the information given — whether it is really impersonal or very personal. If it is personal, it is certainly not from a high level. If it is impersonal, it may be. The higher the guidance, the more impersonal it is. People from all over the world present to me 'guidance' from their guides, their 'Masters', sometimes 'Maitreya'. Without exception, all these messages are from some level of the astral plane. For the most part, they are totally trivial and have no value whatsoever. There exist, of course, books from guides, highly evolved disciples on the higher astral planes, who give, through mediums, very high teaching indeed.

A very clear case is *A Course in Miracles,* inspired by the Master Jesus. It is His concept, His idea, it embodies His teaching, but it was given by one of His disciples on a higher astral plane, through a medium. The Master Jesus Himself would not use a medium in that way. One of His disciples on the inner planes conveyed it through the medium, who was highly evolved, and so *A Course in Miracles* does its work and has behind it the ideas and conceptions of the Master Jesus. That is a very far cry from the usual information which comes through mediums. The Master Jesus is a very high Master, a sixth-degree Initiate, and a close co-worker of Maitreya the Christ. He is involved with all those who pray to Him, who call on Him through the heart rather than from the solar plexus. The heart is the link with Hierarchy, and you can trust the heart and what works through the heart, but you cannot trust what comes through the solar plexus.

How do we know in our own experience the difference between higher psychism and lower psychism?

It is a question of experience and discrimination and a knowledge of your own etheric make-up. You have within yourself a counterpart body to the dense physical, the etheric physical body, made of physical matter of a subtle kind. You can become sensitively aware of your etheric envelope and the centres themselves, as well as where the energy for any given experience is coming from and through which centre it is flowing.

All lower psychic types of activity are activated within the astral levels. There are seven astral planes. These planes are simply states of consciousness, and each has an energy flow. As you become consciously aware of that level, you can utilize its energy. Because humanity has physical plane consciousness, the physical plane is a reality for us. Humanity also has astral (emotional) consciousness, so the astral plane and its energies are available to us, flowing through the solar plexus. When we emote, we are dealing with energy flowing from the astral plane. All lower psychism comes from the astral plane and flows through the solar plexus. When that centre is activated, you know which plane the energy is coming from.

Spiritual energy flows through the heart, throat, and head centres, so anything below the heart you know is lower psychism. Making these distinctions, however, requires a sensitivity to energy and to your own centres, as well as experience, discernment, and detachment.

Are messages and teachings given through mediums valid?

The mediums of the world, in the main, are in communication with some levels of the astral plane. It is the world of glamour and illusion and is built of the thoughtforms of humanity.

There are, of course, many entities out of incarnation who live on the astral plane in their astral vehicles. Some of them communicate through mediums in the world. A great many spiritualists believe that through their medium they get guidance of a superior kind. This guidance, however, can be as spurious as any other kind of communication. The fact that it comes from a non-physical level is no guarantee of its correctness. That is not to say that on the higher (the sixth and seventh) astral planes there are not guides who communicate valuable, uplifting communications of a generalized nature. But never from the astral plane will you get communication of hard facts about the Plan of Hierarchy, because the Masters do not work on that level. The mediums do not know, and the entities who speak through them do not know, the truth or otherwise of the reappearance of the Christ. The Masters do not place within those realms the facts of the Plan. As far as I am concerned, I do not care how gifted the medium, how experienced the transmitter, or how venerable he claims the guide, you will not get that kind of fact from that level. You get teaching of a broad, uplifting, generalized nature, but not hard facts.

Is it likely that 'entities' are giving suggestions on Transmission Meditation different from your advice?

It is possible. There are many mischievous entities on the astral planes who might do that through a mediumistic type. Whatever they bring through should be ignored. It has no bearing on this work, which proceeds from Hierarchy. Information about Transmission Meditation is not available on the astral planes.

Is it likely that those entities could influence the energies?

No, not at all. The energies are under the complete control of the Christ and His group of Masters.

If people do have contact with 'entities' or 'intelligences', where are these entities likely to work?

Without exception on the astral planes, and no notice should be taken of such contacts. People have free will, but if an individual insists on maintaining such contacts, they should be asked to continue their work on their own, outside the Transmission group.

How does that guide process, that mediumship process, differ from the information given by Master D.K. through Alice Bailey?

Totally. The lower psychism works through the apparatus of the personality; the higher psychism works through the apparatus of the soul. Alice Bailey was a very highly evolved individual indeed. She was initiate and used only the soul level of communication, the higher telepathy. D.K. conveyed directly, by the higher telepathy, all that Alice Bailey wrote, except her own books (she wrote five books herself). All the rest were dictated to her precisely by the Master D.K., and she did not alter a word. If she doubted a particular word, He usually said: "Use your judgement in this, your English is better than mine", but sometimes He would say: "No, that's what I mean you to say, use that word." It is as exact and precise as that; it is uncoloured by any quality of the lower mind or the astral body of Alice Bailey. The Hierarchy of Masters, when they wish to convey this kind of teaching, use only those who can function on the soul level, who are sufficiently attuned and at-one with the soul to allow the higher telepathy to take place. That is a very different thing from the work of mediums. Alice Bailey was a mediator, not a medium. You know by the quality of the teaching, the vibration of what comes through — and that is a question of discrimination.

What, if any, is the difference between ordinary telepathy (such as ESP and psychic sensitivity) and the mental telepathy between you and your Master, or between Alice Bailey and the Master D.K.?

Telepathy is a natural human faculty but is as yet largely undeveloped. Most telepathic contacts take place instinctively, haphazardly, as a result of astral action and sensitivity, whereas true telepathy is a mental — mind to mind — process and requires mental polarization to function in a controlled, purposeful fashion.

There is this major difference between true mental (spiritual or soul) telepathy and the more common psychic sensitivity: the latter receives its information (its channelling) from some level of the astral planes. The information or teaching received is, therefore, subject to the illusory nature of those planes (the planes of illusion) and is always, more or less, a distortion of reality. True mental telepathy on the other hand is the direct communication between two fully conscious, focused minds, using the plane of "mind" as the medium through which to make contact. It is really the demonstration of a soul faculty. It is deliberate, instantaneous, and infallible.

The Masters work only from the soul level and use this form of contact between Themselves and those disciples whose mental polarization is sufficiently developed to allow it. There are various degrees of contact and types of relationship between Masters and disciples; this can run all the way from infrequent (and, on the part of the disciple, unconscious) impression, to a moment-to-moment spiritual overshadowing which stops just short of obsession. In this way the disciple's free will is not infringed. Obsession is the method used by the Lords of Materiality (as in the case of Hitler, for example). The Disciple Jesus was deeply overshadowed — but not obsessed — by Maitreya the Christ.

Could you contrast your view of overshadowing with the Biblical view of demonic possession?

They are opposite sides of a coin. There are Masters of the Black Lodge and Masters of the Light. The Masters of whom I am speaking, like the Master Jesus and the Master Morya, for example, Masters of the Hierarchy, are the workers in Light. They work on the consciousness levels with the soul and with Their disciples through various processes relating to the science of impression, the impression of ideas and energy. This ranges all the way from the subtlest kind of mental or astral impression to overshadowing. Overshadowing can be partial and temporary, or more or less total and long term. It can go all the way from the overshadowing of the mental or astral body through the soul to the complete take-over of the physical body. It is a process whereby a more advanced being can manifest some (or all) of his consciousness through a being of lesser degree.

A clear example is the overshadowing of the disciple Jesus by the Christ. The Christ remained in the Himalayas while His consciousness took over and worked through the body of Jesus. This is the classical method for the manifestation of Avatars or Teachers. In no sense was this demonic possession. When the Christ took over the body of Jesus at the Baptism, He did so with the full knowledge, co-operation and assent of the Master Jesus Himself (who was then the disciple Jesus). When the Buddha took over the body of the Prince Gautama, He did so, likewise, with the full consent, approval and co-operation of the Prince. Their free will was never infringed.

With the Black Lodge, on the other hand, this is not the case, and the method of total obsession is often used. On the lower astral planes of this planet, entities exist who do take over the bodies of those who leave themselves open and who have a similarity of vibration. That is demonic possession. It is totally unconscious; there is no conscious design from the point of view of one possesed, and it is, of course, a total infringement of the free will of the individual. It is highly dangerous; to avoid it, keep your vibrational rate at a level above that at which possession can take place.

Spiritual overshadowing takes place either at the Monadic or at the soul level. Maitreya the Christ, is overshadowed at the Monadic level by a Cosmic Avatar called the Spirit of Peace or Equilibrium (in much the same way as He overshadowed Jesus). This spiritual overshadowing, which is an extension of the principle of telepathy, is of quite another order than the usual, spiritualistic overshadowing of a medium by some discarnate entity on the astral planes.

Do the so-called 'forces of darkness' ever impersonate or disguise themselves as the forces of good in order to deceive the well-intentioned, to subvert their intentions? If so, how can we avoid being thus deceived?

Yes, this is a common ploy by the forces of materiality. They often imitate the methods used by the Hierarchy of Light to snare the unwary. The best defense against deception is to examine carefully one's motives and to keep them pure and altruistic. The forces of darkness cannot work or influence where the light and love of the soul dominates the actions. Objectivity and selflessness are the keynotes of soul-inspired actions and ideas. When this is the case, one is automatically protected.

Is my very fear of this a result of 'dark force' activities?

No, it is a common fear. The best thing, to my mind, is to forget entirely the 'dark forces' — proceed as if they did not exist — and thus give them no energy.

A friend has recently become the victim of a psychic attack following a period of intensive inner searching. What is going on here and how can such dangers be avoided? Are there some people for whom deep meditation can be dangerous?

Without knowing the specific circumstances, it is not possible to give other than a general reply to these questions. In the first place, I would be very doubtful that your friend "after intensive inner searching" of the *right* kind became the victim of a psychic 'attack'. Rather, I would suggest, she has upset her own emotional balance by an unskilled approach to meditation. It is not possible to invoke the energies of the soul through meditation and expect to remain the same. There will always be some reaction to these higher energies.

This reaction will normally take one or other of the following courses: if the meditation is scientific and skillfully and sensibly approached, there will be a galvanizing of the person's desire to serve and to create. This may or may not follow a *temporary* period of emotional turmoil as the soul energies affect the astral body. If the meditation chosen is unsuitable or wrongly practised — that is, without due care and a sense of proportion — the result can be very unfortunate, especially if the person is emotionally unstable in the first place. I would suggest that this is the problem with your friend. Psychic 'attacks' do occur but seldom to people engaged seriously in meditation. They generally occur to people, mediumistic in nature, who leave themselves open, through similarity of vibration, to interference from the lower astral planes. The way to avoid such dangers is to keep the aspiration and vibrational rate as high as possible through meditation and service.

I think I am attracting bad vibrations from people around me through their dislike, jealousy, etc., and this is making me ill. Is this likely to be so?

Ninety-nine times out of a hundred this is not the case. The various diseases from which people suffer are almost always the result of their own emotional imbalance, misuse of energy from the soul, mental or astral planes — that is, they are karmic reactions. Of course, there are a few cases in which there is an outside cause, but these are so few as to be ignored for the most part. It is wiser and more accurate, usually, not to blame other people for one's physical ills. The thing is to aim at mental control of the emotional body and detachment from one's emotions, and thus to strengthen one's aura.

During Transmission Meditation, do we need special protection or are the Masters protecting us from outside or bad influences?

During a Transmission Meditation, the Masters are in complete control of this energetic process and *everyone* taking part is totally protected from any outside source. They do not, however, protect anyone from their own astral imaginings.

I am in a Transmission group and, in the course of my work (with industrial machinery), I am subjected daily to high noise and vibrational levels. Can this adversely affect the etheric body and the quality of one's Transmission Meditation? If so, is there any way I can protect myself? (I have tried keeping my attention on the ajna centre while I work.)

Loud and sustained noise levels can certainly affect the etheric body but not, I think, the quality of one's Transmission Meditation. I know of no way in which you can protect yourself beyond learning to 'go with' the noise rather than resisting it.

What is the difference between imagination and true inner knowing?

Inner knowing is intuition. What we call intuition really comes not from the intuitional level, but from the Manasic level. The soul is the receptor for three spiritual levels stemming from the Monad or Spirit, of which the soul is the reflection. We are really threefold. That reality must never be forgotten. We must get used to seeing ourselves as the soul.

The difference between inner knowing and imagination is a question of focus of consciousness. Most people are focused on the astral plane. They function through the solar plexus, and their knowing is emotional and astral. That is imagination. In the esoteric terminology, there is a state called glamour. We have an inkling of it when we say "the glamour of Hollywood". The glamour of Hollywood suggests it is all marvellous, but it is also called Tinsel Town. We know it is unreal, however interesting or emotionally appealing. That which stems from the astral planes is unreal. Our emotional reactions are the result of the energy of the astral plane flowing through the solar plexus. Glamour is illusion on the astral plane.

The evolutionary aim of humanity is to work from the mental planes. You have to become mentally focused to control the astral plane. The astral plane is meant to be a mirror, a still lake, on which the inner knowing, the spiritual intuition of the Buddhic level can reflect itself. When the astral body is still and purified, it no longer reacts to the movement of astral energy through it. While the astral body remains unpurified, it causes chaos: we are tossed in a storm of astral energy, and it makes us behave in all sorts of totally irrelevant, irresponsible, and unreal ways, because the astral plane is, literally, unreal. For the Masters it does not exist. It is illusion, whereas buddhi, the spiritual intuition, is the inner knowing. When truly creative people in any field say "by the use of the imagination", they really mean by the use of the intuition. That is a very different thing from what we call imagination, which stems from the astral and is not really imagination, but fantasy.

Intuition is straight knowledge: knowing because you know. It comes from the Buddhic level, and it is always right. It can never be wrong, because it comes through the soul — from above the level of the soul — but through the soul. It becomes available to humanity when the emotional body is purified and controlled. As soon as that happens, the energy which would otherwise play through the emotional body is transmuted, lifted up to the heart. Of course, it is a long and gradual process. Heart reaction is always correct. You can always trust the reaction of the heart under every circumstance.

The trouble is that most people's reactions, even if only in part, come also from the solar plexus. That brings in glamour. So although they have the intention of doing their best, the activity of the solar plexus renders it, at least to some extent, glamour. People live in glamour. I know many people who believe they are the Christ. They write to me all the time. They ring me on the telephone. They even come to my door. They experience the feeling that they are *the* One. That is glamour.

Intuition is absolutely direct. You know instantaneously, and it never fails. It functions through the heart without any admixture of emotional energy. The difference between pity and compassion is the difference between glamour and a true intuitive heart, a Buddhic reaction. You can feel it in your centres, if you are aware of your centres. Wherever the activity of the solar plexus centre is informing your experience, it will be glamour. If it is purely and simply from the heart centre, then you can trust it.

CHAPTER VIII

SOUL, MEDITATION AND SERVICE

You said that we need to make use of the energies which come to us in meditation. What do you mean? What is the real purpose of meditation?

Meditation is a method, more or less scientific (depending on the meditation), for bringing the man or woman in incarnation into contact and eventual at-one-ment with the Higher Self or soul.

The time has passed for meditating alone, getting on with one's own personal spiritual salvation, without at the same time accepting the need, the duty, of service. The nature of the soul is to serve. The soul knows only altruistic service and comes into incarnation to serve. So what is the point, as a meditator, of spending all that time and effort getting into touch with the soul and not carrying out its purpose? The soul is carrying out the Plan of the Logos. It is a great sacrifice for the soul to do so, because it is so limited at this physical level. It gains experience at this level, but the true reason behind the incarnating process is the carrying out of the Will of the Logos through the sacrificial decision of the soul itself.

When the soul pours its energy into the vehicles — physical, emotional/astral and mental — these vehicles are stimulated; the soul seeks to grip the personality and turn it into a reflection of itself. The personality senses this and resists. Then there follows several lives of a long, drawn-out battle between the personality, with its powerful desire nature, and the soul. The soul inevitably wins because it is a higher agency; its energy is stronger and the law of evolution is working behind it. Eventually it will turn that personality into a reflection of itself. But it can only do so when the personality gives in and begins to reflect the quality of the soul. Then the Spiritual Will, the Spiritual Love, and the higher mental nature can reflect through the personality, and the man or woman becomes a living soul.

All those who have engaged in meditation will have been engaged, whether they know it or not, in aligning the physical brain with the soul, the personality vehicle with the Higher Self. That is what meditation is for.

When we meditate and do not use the soul energy in purposeful service, the result is always some disturbance of the equilibrium of the energies in the etheric body. The centres get blocked; the result is inevitably neurosis or physical plane illness of some kind. This is why you find so many more advanced people rather neurotic. They dam up the energy coming to them from the soul level. They do this by not using that energy in service. They use it selfishly — in other words, they misuse it. This is a stage we all go through and there is no condemnation involved. The way to avoid neurosis is to use soul energy correctly. It is the most effective way to avoid neurosis and other illnesses, apart from those, of course, which are karmic, stemming from our past.

Does Transmission Meditation lead us to Hierarchy? Will it help speed up the process of mental polarization?

Transmission work is a door which leads to a path that takes you directly to Hierarchy. It is part of a process planned by Hierarchy whereby the aspirants and the disciples of the world will work in a co-operative fashion with each other.

Most people want to approach Hierarchy whether they are ready for it or not — they would like to meet and work with a Master. Transmission is not a way to meet Masters, but it is certainly the simplest way to work with the Masters.

What we are really doing in Transmission Meditation (besides helping the world) is doing Kriya Yoga, which is actually being done for you by the Masters. Gradually, the shifting of the point of polarization from astral to mental is taking place, without your being aware of it. What you do become aware of is the change in yourself, in your outlook on the world. Many people have said to me: "I feel a better person; I can do my work better; I am more mentally focused, more articulate; I can bring many ideas together, . . .", and so on. This is all the result of steady Transmission work. It happens just by doing Transmission, because it is being done for you by the Masters. It is a deeply occult meditation, and the Masters manipulate the energy for you. What you might achieve in 20 years of Kriya Yoga practice, you will probably achieve in one year of steady Transmission work.

Mental polarization is the result of a shift in consciousness from the astral/emotional plane to the mental plane. It covers the period between the first and second initiations (an average of six to seven lives), and starts at a point half-way between these two great events (planetary initiations). Being mentally polarized allows the soul to work through the mental plane and destroy the glamour of astral plane activity. When the fogs of glamour are dispersed by the light of the mental plane, a gradual shift in polarization takes place.

Many people confuse the emotional and mental processes. They imagine they are 'thinking' when in fact they are clothing their emotional reactions in astral thoughtforms which they mistake for 'thoughts'. Anything, therefore, which focuses the mind, which brings it into action in every situation or reaction, speeds the process of polarization. Meditation, of whatever kind (except that state of negative reverie which is so often mistaken for meditation), is a prime mover in this direction; a diligent determination to look, as impersonally and honestly as possible, at all one's reactions, in every situation, especially the most disturbing; an understanding of one's ray structure — and therefore of one's glamours; a dedication of one's life to service to humanity, leading to greater decentralization; all of these help to shift the consciousness onto the higher plane, thus bringing the light of the soul into each life situation.

Is correct Transmission Meditation alone sufficient for humans to elevate themselves, or is it also necessary to work out one's emotions through analysis?

Done with consistency and application, Transmission Meditation will gradually bring about the mental polarization which alone leads to emotional control. Of course, service of all kinds, which tends towards de-centralization of the self, aids in this. I would not think that analysis, unless for some painfully neurotic condition, would be necessary. Analysis frequently focuses the attention too firmly on the self.

Is Transmission Meditation sufficient in the field of service, or should other forms of service come with it?

Transmission Meditation will be sufficient for the whole of your service life, if you apply yourself sufficiently to it. But there is a world out there to save, and a thousand different ways to serve. It need not be the totality of service. You will find that whatever else you do — any other form of meditation, of service, of activity — will be potentized by doing Transmission Meditation.

What aspect of meditation eventually makes one cope with all the pain experienced in the world, without being totally oversensitive to all the world suffering?

It is true that not only Transmission Meditation but all meditation will sensitize the instrument — the man or woman in incarnation — because it imbues the personality with some of the qualities of the soul, such as its spiritual sensitivity and love nature. As this process takes place, what should also be taking place is a growing sense of spiritual detachment — not indifference, or even impersonality, which are not spiritual qualities at all, but are simply the separative experience of the personality. What is needed is the utmost immediate sensitive response to the pain, the suffering, the needs of the world, and at the same time a spiritual detachment from emotional reaction to that pain and suffering, to enable action to be taken on behalf of humanity. If the identification with the pain and suffering is such as to make action impossible, it is simply an emotional self-indulgence. The soul sees all the pain and suffering; the Christ, who is the embodied soul of humanity, sees the pain and suffering but has such spiritual detachment, is so lacking in emotional reaction, that He can work in the most potent way.

You have to differentiate between a heart/love response to pain and suffering, with a spiritual detachment which allows you to act on its behalf, and an emotional reaction which locks you into that pain and suffering. Love is active. An emotional reaction is simply sentimentality. It is identification, seeing one's own suffering. It is because you see the suffering in yourself that you identify with the outer. A love response has no sense of its own suffering, so it can identify without reacting emotionally. It is a question of identifying with the needs of the world without undergoing the emotional reactions.

What is the importance of group work, and in what way does Transmission Meditation help group activities?

The New Age is the age of group consciousness, not simply working together as a group, but thinking and feeling and experiencing together in group consciousness, total oneness. This is unknown to humanity as yet. The Masters of the Wisdom, on the other hand, have *only* group consciousness. The separate self does not exist in Their consciousness. Working together in groups gives humanity experience in developing that group consciousness.

Humanity itself, of course, is the major 'group'. We are all part of that group. At the moment we live separated and divided lives, but in this coming time we shall work as a group. In fact, if we do not, if we cannot realize and express, through our structures and institutions, the inner unity or group reality of humanity, we shall destroy ourselves.

We are beginning to understand that the work of any kind of activity goes forward better in groups. The first thing that I was asked to do, when I began my public work, was to form a Transmission group. There is a good reason for that. At the base of every really active group in this work, there is a Transmission group; that is the source of the energy. The spiritual nourishment comes into the group from the Masters — you have a power base there, a fountain from which you can drink all the time.

Not every group has this. Many are responding in a vaguer way to the energies which are being sent out, but they may not have a powerful dynamic process that keeps them continually spiritually charged to enable them to do their work with maximum intensity. So many tend to be 'talky-talky' groups that often disband quickly or reform and change their activities, partly out of a natural process of growth, but also partly because of the demand for change for its own sake. But when you have a Transmission group as the basis of all activity, you have an inflow of energy which is constant. It is like being tuned in to the electricity the whole time, so you always have the fire on if you need it. That is one of the important things in groups doing Transmission work.

Which is the best kind of meditation for the new age?

There is no simple answer to this question. It depends on the individual's point in evolution, ray structure, background, tradition, and so on.

Meditations of all kinds are methods, more or less scientific depending on the meditation, of achieving soul contact and eventual at-one-ment. In the new age, group activity will be the main method of work and service. Group meditation will therefore become increasingly the norm. For those with a strong desire to serve, Transmission Meditation provides the most potent and scientific vehicle for service with, at the same time, the most powerful stimulus to personal growth.

Will there be new meditation techniques given by Maitreya? Will they be different from existing ones?

No. It will not be Maitreya's function to give new meditation techniques. That is like expecting the managing director of a large international company to train the office boys in office routine. Meditation techniques are, and will continue to be, taught by disciples of the Masters. As time goes on and disciples become ready, meditation forms will be given by the Masters Themselves, working exoterically.

Is the healing process known as 'laying on of hands' related to alignment of the chakras?

Yes. All energy entering the body comes into the etheric vehicle through the chakras. In laying on of hands, the energy moves through the chakras in the palms of the healer into the patient. The source of the energy depends on the evolution of the healer. Most commonly, it comes from the solar plexus centre of the healer, from his or her own life force. It often involves energy that the healer has invoked from his or her own soul, and sometimes also from the soul of the patient, which will augment the energy of the physical body. There are also many healers who work under guidance, consciously or unconsciously, from some higher source. Some disciples on the inner planes, and even Masters, work through certain individuals, without the individual necessarily being aware of it. The aim is always the removal of stasis and the correct balance of the chakras.

How does one obtain healing powers?

I believe at least 70 per cent of people have the potential to transmit healing energies from some source or other, usually from their own soul. Meditation, service, and practice are the key methods of strengthening and fulfilling that potential.

How can I get rid of negativities in my life so more light can come in?

There is no finer way to get rid of negativity than to serve, to use the light coming in. As you serve, you begin to identify with what you serve, so you begin a process of becoming decentralized. As you become more decentralized, less egotistical, less the central point in your life, you become more objective, broader in view, increasingly identified with all that is. You identify first with yourself, that is easy. Then you identify with your family and with your friends, and then in a patriotic way with your country, and then more objectively with the planet as a whole, and finally with all of the cosmos. As you do this you expand your identity — not just your intellectual awareness, but your heart identity — until there is no sense of separation, until you and the cosmos are one. Then you are perfect, as the Masters are perfect.

Many people, during their practice of meditation, spontaneously find their hands and bodies assuming positions that are called 'mudras' in the Hindu tradition. Swami Muktananda wrote a great deal about his own experiences of this kind. Often the meditator has no idea until afterwards that for thousands of years these identical positions have been a part of Hindu, Buddhist, and even Christian traditions. How does this happen? What makes it happen at some times and not others?

This is an interesting phenomenon which personally I have experienced many times. In meditation, a person is brought into contact, more or less, depending on the meditation and experience of the meditator, with his or her own soul. When holding a mudra takes place involuntarily, one of three things has happened: either the soul itself has impressed its vehicle to strengthen the value of the meditation by 'locking in' or distributing the soul energy invoked, or there is a spontaneous repetition, from a previous life, of an older pattern of meditation practice. In cases (which of course are much rarer) where the meditator is in conscious contact with a Master or high initiate, these latter may impress the use of mudras on the mind of the disciple during the meditation.

During Transmission Meditation is it helpful to use certain mudras (hand positions)?

No. If it were helpful, it would already be suggested. Keep Transmission Meditation as simple as possible — as it is presented.

Could you tell me if icons are a good focus for meditation, and something about their significance, for instance, the austere facial expressions of the subjects depicted? Also, were the artists inspired in some way while creating them?

Icons come out of the Byzantine tradition and are indeed meant as a focus for meditation, worship, and prayer. They have been used as such for centuries. The austere facial expressions are meant to symbolize the holiness and other-worldliness of the divine subject matter. Icons have remained unchanged in style for many centuries (like Egyptian art) and have been created by artists of all levels and degrees of inspiration, from the great to the mediocre. They would only be useful in meditation if one 'believed' in the divinity of the subjects and that they could be contacted through the icon.

How can one remove the veil of ignorance from one's mind so that true communion can occur during meditation or prayer?

The 'veil of ignorance' is the result of wrong identification, with the separate personality rather than with the soul. The way to soul expression (and true communion) is, as always, through correct meditation and service.

What does Shanti mean?

Peace.

(1) The Lucis Trust Triangle Newsletter reports that, according to the Academy for Peace Research in Massachusetts, there is a 36 per cent drop in solar activity averages for two weeks after a

global peace meditation. (2) They quote research that states since 1900, violent behaviour patterns and disease patterns have been correlated with increase in sun-spot activity. Is this true or wishful thinking?

(1) Wishful thinking. There is no way in which a peace meditation, global or otherwise, can affect sun-spot activity, which is cyclic in nature. (2) True. The increased energy resulting from sun-spot activity does indeed produce results of tension (and, often, therefore, of violence and disease) in humanity.

As a young child of seven or thereabouts living in the countryside, when gazing after dark at individual stars, I would feel a shaft of sweetness, love, and beauty coming apparently from the star I was looking at. As an adult I find this no longer happens. Would you know if children are open to some influence from stars, and if so, what is this influence?

Be ye as little children! Yes, indeed, the stars do radiate most beneficent energies of love and synthesis and beauty and many children (and, of course, some adults) are sensitive to this 'star-dust'.

Living in electrically-lit cities, most people do not even see the stars. Those fortunate enough to live in areas where the stars' energies can be experienced should make use of this high radiation and speed their progress to the stars themselves. Look up, and accept the radiance of the Blessed Pleiades as a gift from the Gods.

CHAPTER IX

MAINTAINING ALIGNMENT

This chapter focuses on how to maintain the alignment between the physical brain and the soul, a prerequisite for proper Transmission of spiritual energies. This subject was discussed in detail at the 1990 Tara network conferences held in San Francisco, USA and Veldhoven, Holland. Benjamin Creme's talks at these conferences dealt with discipleship and practice, the true meaning of discipleship, and the need for greater commitment to practise the teaching given. The talk and discussions which followed were published in Maitreya's Mission, Vol. II, pp. 480-494. The portions of these discussions which relate to Transmission Meditation are reprinted here.

DISCIPLESHIP AND PRACTICE

IT IS A TRUISM in occultism that no new teaching can be given until that already given has been put into practice. This is a law. You cannot take in anything higher until you have put into practice what you have already received. Mainly, people approach esotericism as if it were an academic subject in which you take exams and get a degree. It is not like that at all. Certainly there are degrees — degrees of initiation — but you can become an initiate without knowing anything about esoteric theory or practice at all, by living naturally, intuitively, the life of a disciple.

You have to do it one way or the other. You can do it intuitively, or through the acquiring of knowledge and the application of the rules and precepts in your life, moment to moment. It is an all-day affair. In my experience, most people set about being a disciple in a very lukewarm way. They fit it into their everyday life when there is a moment to spare. The average disciple does not realize that the disciple is a different person from the rest of humanity. The rules and laws which apply, even the laws of cause and effect and of rebirth, which affect humanity willy-nilly, affect the disciple differently, according to his ability to work within them and to manipulate them to the soul's needs.

A disciple, or anyone who aspires to become a disciple, must recognize first of all that he is an ordinary human being who has made a pledge and has taken in hand the development of his own evolution. He is learning to work with the soul and to carry out its purpose. Whatever other purposes the soul may have, under the Law of Sacrifice its purpose is to work with the Plan of evolution in so far as the disciple can intuit it and put it into effect in his or her life. Only the rudiments of the plan may become real in his or her consciousness, but in so far as these aspects do become real, it behooves him or her to put them into effect in life. Actually doing this is very rare indeed.

It is not the forces of evil that worry the Christ and the Masters of the Hierarchy. They can cope with the forces of evil rather well. Most people think that the main obstacles to the externalization of the Hierarchy and the spiritualization of the life of humanity are the problems involved with the forces of materiality. There are such problems. But some of the quickest responders to that materiality are the disciples of the world. It is the ingrained materiality and, above all, inertia of disciples as well as everyone else that keeps humanity in thrall to the forces of materiality, the forces of evil as we call them.

Disciples are doubly responsible. They have the responsibility of ordinary humanity plus extra responsibility because they know some aspects of the truth. They have taken upon themselves to do something about changing the situation in the world, and to change their own nature in such a way as to work intelligently with the Plan. Yet people are so steeped in materialism — it is so ingrained in the vast body of even the world's disciples — that little or no action is taken by any of us to remedy the situation. We remain as engrossed in materialism as anyone else. That is the problem for the Christ and the

Masters: not the forces of evil, but the inertia, the crippling inertia of the disciples of the world.

I learned recently from my Master that the average number of minutes in which people in the Transmission Meditation groups around the world are actually aligned, in which the physical brain and the soul are aligned — so that they are being transmitted through and therefore doing the work of Transmission — is astonishingly small.

Why is this? There has to be a reason why, after 10 years, you are still doing so poorly. This is the 10th year in which I have come to the United States and the 10th year in which some of you have been doing Transmission Meditation.

"What have you been doing all these years?" I ask myself. Of course it is a question of polarization. If one is astrally polarized — and the majority of people in these groups are — it is more difficult to hold the attention at the ajna centre and so be aligned for longer than a few minutes at a time. Also people do not seem to know the difference between being aligned and not being aligned. They really think they are aligned. I am sure all of you are shocked by this statement. You imagine you are aligned yet, quite frankly, most of the time you are not.

What are you doing if you are not aligned? I suggest that you are in a state of reverie. You are ruminating. You are in a state in which your attention is hovering around the solar plexus. But since you know that Transmission Meditation involves focusing your attention at the ajna centre, and since from time to time, when you remember, you can bring the attention back there, you forget that it has dropped. But within a few minutes it has dropped. If you add up the few minutes in which it is really held at the ajna centre and in which you are transmitting, it comes to, on average, four to five minutes in the hour. Some people do only an hour's Transmission in the week. That is four to five minutes in the week. It is not a lot. 'The Role of Transmission Meditation in the Development of the Disciple' [the title of a previous talk, printed in Chapter X. *Ed.*] is something which does not apply to people who are doing four or five minutes' actual Transmission in the week. Little can be expected to happen in that time.

Nevertheless, enough happens to make Transmission Meditation a powerful way to serve. If you are transmitting four or five minutes in the hour even for only one hour a week, you are receiving the benefit of these spiritual forces through the chakras in a way still more powerful than you would have achieved by any other method, given the same amount of time and effort.

The point is, people do not make much effort. They think they do. They mean well. Everyone means well. Everyone imagines that they are working quite hard. But from a Master's point of view, they are only playing at being in a Transmission group, playing at helping the world. A Transmission Meditation group contacts spiritual energies which transform the whole world, politically, economically, socially, and so on. Most people are contributing to this for only a few minutes a week, yet they feel that they are in a very potent, powerful situation — which they are — but only because these energies are so potent, so powerful, are these short minutes of actual Transmission worth anything at all.

SOUL ALIGNMENT

We have been doing Transmission Meditation for quite some time now, but it seems we have not been able to do it correctly (i.e. be aligned). Have we not been really serving through Transmission Meditation?

I know people who are very happy and proud to be in a Transmission Meditation group. They talk about it, tell their friends about it, and sometimes write to me about it. Then I find out that they are doing perhaps an hour, or even half an hour, a week. Before they start, they have, perhaps, a study group, do exercises, hold healing sessions, etc. After it, they have cake, coffee, and chat with their friends. In between they put in half an hour or an hour of Transmission Meditation and, in so doing, they think they are serving the Plan. It is really a major glamour. If you are actually aligned for perhaps five minutes in an hour (the average), it is really not very much. Five minutes per hour once a week is hardly serving the Plan of evolution. It is pretending to serve the Plan of evolution. I say this with feeling because I know that many people attend Transmission Meditation in a very casual way: not even every week, perhaps once every two, three, or four weeks. Still, they think of themselves as doing Transmission Meditation. That is their service activity, once a week, or once a month for an hour or a couple of hours at the most, in which they might be aligned, and therefore actually transmitting, for five minutes.

I make a big point of this because it is very important to realize that if you are not aligned, you are not transmitting. The energies proceed from the soul level and you have to be aligned with your soul. That is why you have to hold the attention at the ajna centre. If you do not do that, but look around, or think about what you had for dinner and how it is sitting heavily in your stomach, then most likely you are not aligned at all. Most people have very poor attention and therefore very poor alignment. Having said all that, the saving grace, however, is that Transmission Meditation is so powerful, so scientific, that even these few minutes are more valuable in terms of service and personal growth than anything else you might do.

The Japanese groups, I have to say, have a completely different attitude to Transmission Meditation and to service in general. It is probably due to the 6th-ray soul of Japan and the long tradition which the Japanese have in relation to meditation. They take to Transmission Meditation like ducks to water, as we say. They love it, are good at it, and they hold the world's record for alignment during Transmission and therefore for actually transmitting. The average alignment time in the world is around five or six minutes. There are some, of course, who do very much more. There are people in Japan who do 55 minutes in an hour, and most will be aligned for 10 minutes in an hour. The average in Japan is around 15 to 20 minutes per hour. That is real transmitting.

How can one be sure of true alignment?

There is one way to be sure of true alignment. That is to become mentally polarized. If you are not mentally polarized, you will find it more difficult to maintain alignment. True alignment is the result of a constant polarization and focus on the mental plane or higher.

Humanity is going through a process of gradually lifting its seat of consciousness, the general level where its consciousness acts, from the astral to the mental planes. For six million years, during the first, the Lemurian, race, the consciousness of humanity was focused on the physical plane. There is no one in the world today who has only physical plane consciousness. We have awareness on that plane, so it has reality for us, but it is not the seat of our consciousness.

For the bulk of humanity, the seat of consciousness has moved up to the astral plane. This shift of focus was achieved by man during the Atlantean root race, which lasted 12 million years. It took, therefore, a long time for Atlantean man to perfect the astral vehicle, which he did to such good effect that the majority of people today are still polarized on the astral plane. The astral is the most powerful body of the average individual.

We are members of the fifth, or Aryan, root race (which has nothing to do with Hitler's idea of Aryan). We have as an evolutionary goal the perfecting of the mental vehicle, which results when a person has consciousness on all four of the mental planes (there are four sub-planes of the mental as there are seven sub-planes of the astral). When you have achieved polarization on these and have lifted your consciousness up to the causal plane (the highest sub-plane of the mental plane), you have the beginning of spiritual polarization.

In terms of initiation, astral polarization, and therefore astral focus of consciousness, continues until half-way between the first and second initiations — what I call 1.5. For convenience, my Master and I have agreed upon this definition of exactitude in talking about a person's point in evolution. You get a very fine gradation of degree, which means level of consciousness, if you do it that way.

At around 1.5, the shift from astral to mental polarization begins to take place. If you are 1.5, you will probably still be astrally polarized, although from time to time there will be a degree of mental polarization. An oscillation between astral and mental takes place for quite a long time until 1.6. Then you can say that person is mentally polarized, even if only at the beginning of mental polarization. It may be interesting to note that the majority of our present world leaders are around 1.6, so they have the beginnings of mental polarization. They are obviously advanced members of humanity, but from the point of view of the Masters, they are still in the elementary stages of discipleship.

At 1.6 you can begin to function in the world in an altogether more powerful way. As soon as you achieve mental polarization, as soon as you can work on the mental plane intelligently, your influence, power, and input into the world are increased, as the Master D.K. put it, a hundredfold. Such is the difference between astral and mental polarization that moving from 1.5 to 1.6 gives you a hundredfold more power, influence, and effect in the world — so powerful is the mental plane compared with the astral.

Mental polarization continues until half-way between the second and third initiations. At that point the polarization shifts from the mental plane to the soul level, and the alignment is complete. It may oscillate for some time, but eventually there is steady spiritual polarization. The person is then aligned automatically all the time. There is no effort made to hold the alignment. We do not make any effort to have consciousness on the physical or astral plane; it is natural for us. It is only when it comes to the mental plane that many people have a problem. The spiritual plane for most people is only an idea, something they might touch on in a meditation, but not much more than that.

How can you be sure of true alignment? Become mentally polarized and eventually, of course, spiritually polarized — in other words, become initiate.

How can we recognize that we are actually aligned during a Transmission? How do we know?

It may be that some people cannot know. The person who is very astrally polarized, whose emotional body is highly excited and therefore disruptive of their focus, will most likely not have the attention to discover what alignment is. Alignment between the personality and the soul takes place when you can hold your attention at the ajna centre between the eyebrows. This is the directing centre. Eventually it becomes the synthesis for all the centres below it.

If you are still very astrally polarized, you may not have much attention. The recognition of alignment, and practically everything else in development of any kind, is to do with attention. If you do not have the attention, you do not learn much. If you are teaching a child and the child does not pay attention, he does not learn. You only learn that to which you give your attention. If you want to learn very well, to make the utmost use of the time and energy you give to any job, do it with full, total attention to the exclusion of everything else, totally concentrated and attending to what you are doing.

When someone is talking to you and you really want to know what they are saying (and are not just being polite and thinking your own thoughts), you have to give them attention. When you give them attention, you hear — and usually remember. Likewise, you can recognize the chakras, you can feel whether you are aligned or not, only when you pay attention to what is happening. During a Transmission Meditation, the energies from Hierarchy are going through the various chakras. If your attention is held at the ajna centre, an alignment is automatically created between the physical brain and the soul, using the channel of light we call the antahkarana.

You would not be doing Transmission Meditation if you had not done some form of meditation before this life. All of you have done much meditation in previous lives, perhaps the last four or five, in which you formed, to a considerable degree of efficiency, the antahkarana. That channel is made of energy and connects the soul and the brain of the man or woman. Through it, the alignment between soul and brain is maintained. As soon as you put your attention on the ajna centre, you activate that channel. If you do not pay attention to what is happening to you, you do not become aware. The whole of life, you will find, the whole of development, is a process by which you gradually become aware of more and more. It is a gradual perfecting of an instrument of awareness. In Transmission Meditation, it is an instrument through which the energies are sent out to the world. In the same way, it is an instrument by which the Self can demonstrate Itself, manifest on the physical plane, because that is the nature of the service taking place through the soul. The soul acts in service to the Self. The personality eventually has to act in service to the soul.

Are there some basic rules for alignment and for knowing when you are aligned, or does it vary according to the rays, body sensitivity, etc.?

It certainly varies according to bodily sensitivity. There are some physical bodies seemingly made of wood or stone, quite insensitive to the energies flowing through the etheric body.

Not everyone knows they have an etheric body. They have heard that everyone has an etheric body, but as far as their experience goes, they are not aware of it. This is very much a matter of physical, not mental or personality, ray. It can be partly (but only partly) to do with actual level of evolution. In groups like these, that is not usually the case because everyone is around the same level, more or less. It is largely that they have this wooden- or mineral-type body which makes them literally insensitive to their physical experience and therefore it does not register in the brain. There is some dichotomy between their physical sensation and the ability of the computer system which is their brain to register it. It does not mean they are less evolved.

Are there some basic rules for alignment? The first rule is to pay attention. Make the concentrated effort of holding the attention at the ajna centre. It does not happen by itself. If you have the will to perform well in Transmission Meditation, and to become a better instrument for the Masters in this way, you have to implement your will. Make the necessary effort. Practise. Hold the attention at the ajna centre. Practise holding it there all the time during the day. And do not keep interrupting and distracting your attention; a positive mental focus is required.

During Transmission Meditation, should we pay attention to the energies coming into the body, feeling the physical plane, or should we just focus on the ajna centre and not bother about sensing the energies in the physical body?

It depends on the type of body you have. Some people have a very strong experience of the energies on the physical plane, in the etheric body. There are those who experience the energies in one way or another, but who say they don't actually feel them, in the physical sense of the word. It would be useless to tell these people to concentrate on the energies on the physical plane, because they don't experience the energies there. If you do experience the energies on the physical plane, clearly and strongly, and your attention is focused on the ajna centre, I don't see how you cannot be aware of them, even without focusing on them.

For myself, I am totally aware of the experience on the physical plane, in the etheric chakras, of the different energies as they come in. I differentiate between one and another, or what the particular blend is. I am overshadowed by Maitreya, and He is releasing the energy of the Cosmic Triangle. He brings it down the planes, and then takes it up the planes. Perhaps the Avatar of Synthesis will be at a certain level, the Spirit of Peace at another level, the Buddha at another level. Maitreya takes the energies up and down, and I watch this taking place. I am not saying that therefore everybody should watch, but if you do watch what your etheric body is experiencing, you can in time begin to differentiate between the different types of energy, each of which is unique. At the beginning of Transmission, I mention the energies as they come in, whether the Cosmic Triangle or the ray energies, so that people can learn to distinguish between one and another. On the other hand, it is perfectly possible for people to transmit efficiently without recognizing one energy from another.

During Transmission Meditation I sometimes cannot feel the ajna centre, even though my mind is still and I feel my attention is in the right neighborhood. Does this mean (1) I am definitely not aligned, or (2) could I still be aligned but just insensitive to the etheric body?

(1) No, not necessarily. (2) Yes.

I do not know if I am aligned in a Transmission Meditation. Somehow it seems I am not, except for a few minutes in an hour. What is missing?

What is missing is attention. And awareness. Pay attention to what is actually happening, to what you are experiencing as the energies are sent, with your attention held at the ajna centre.

You will become aware of activity in this chakra. You may become aware of activity in other chakras, too, of a vibration of energy, a kind of pressure as the energies flow through the chakras. Every time you take part in a Transmission, the chakras are expanded more than they were before. The energies stimulate the chakras' activity and radiate out to the world, and

143

you should try to become aware of that energy actually flowing through the chakra.

When you are not aligned, when your attention drops, as it inevitably does, you may go on feeling energy and think you are still aligned. But 99 times out of 100 you are simply feeling the residual vibration of the energy after it has passed through the chakra. While you are aligned, there is a dynamic movement through the chakra, but as soon as you stop being aligned, the energy is no longer being sent through you. The energy comes from the soul plane, but if you are not in touch with the soul plane through the alignment, you cannot be receiving the energy.

You have to recognize that this is so by paying attention. Recognize the difference between a dynamic flow of energy through the chakra and simply a residual vibration which exists after the energy has passed through.

Are you saying that we have to become sensitive to the etheric body to recognize if we are aligned with our soul and properly transmitting?

That is a prerequisite. The dense physical comes from the etheric physical which underlies it. The chakras exist not in the dense but in the etheric physical.

Therefore, if you want to become aware of the chakras, and so become more sensitive to the coming and going of energies and of different types of energy — because they all feel different — you have to become aware of the etheric body.

If we are not aware of the chakras during a Transmission, is it likely that we are not properly transmitting?

You can recognize when you are aligned and properly transmitting if you are experiencing the flow of energy through the chakra. You actually feel the pulse of energy. If you are not aware of the chakra, it is possible that you are not actually aligned and not transmitting. You may find that your attention is down at the solar plexus. Many people do not feel this chakra either, but since most people are astrally polarized, it is the regular seat of their consciousness and therefore attention, so they do not even need to feel it. But you can learn to feel this (solar plexus) chakra too.

It is a very powerful chakra, a distributing centre, and you can absorb energy from the sun through it and charge yourself every day. You can close it (and so not waste your energy), work with it scientifically. When you are aware of the chakra, you will find that you can open and close it at will, but you have to become aware of it first of all as a functioning unit in your etheric body. Then it will obey your will; whatever you tell it to do, it will do.

Is it possible to ruminate in your head and think that you are focused on the ajna centre?

It is not only possible, it happens all the time. That is why some people do three or four minutes of real Transmission in the hour. Thinking they are focused on the ajna centre, they are in fact ruminating. Rumination and reverie are astral activities. Reverie is one of the main obstacles to correct Transmission, to any kind of meditation for that matter. A great many people mistake reverie for meditation, and believe that the astral imaginings which they experience in that state are promptings from the soul or messages from Masters or even Archangels, while they are only subconscious musings.

Reverie, rumination, going through those satisfying imaginary experiences, inhibits correct thinking. More and more, the race has to learn to use the mental body, of which we have barely scratched the surface. Therefore, it is essential to lift your consciousness out of the astral morass into the light of the mind through which the soul can work. Bring your mind, and the will behind it, to bear on these astral, glamourous imaginings and reverie and dry them up at the source.

Define exactly the mental activity we can and can't have during Transmission. Are there symbols we can visualize or focus on?

There are certainly not symbols you should visualize or focus on. The mental activity you can have during Transmission is any level that does not interfere with your alignment. You will have found, no doubt, that any level at all interferes with your alignment. Ideally, you should be so constantly aligned that you can talk, write, whatever, and still continue in an absolute alignment. It should become as instinctual, as self-maintaining as that.

Since few have that kind of focus, you have to limit the activity of the mental body. That happens automatically when you hold your attention at the ajna centre. If you think OM, there is not much else you can think at the same time. If you think OM, you will find that immediately all the thinking that you were doing before subsides. Your attention is aligned, until you lose it and the whole thing starts up again: the monkey mind becomes active and your attention drops again. When you recognize that, sound OM and you will find that for a time, perhaps seconds or minutes, you are suddenly in another tranquil, more blissful state in which there is no mental activity. It is not necessary to get rid of all mental activity in order to be aligned, but for most people mental activity is a hindrance to alignment.

How can I deal with physical discomfort during a Transmission?

Find a comfortable, upright chair and use a cushion if necessary. If you are really aligned, you will not be too aware of your physical sensations. You will feel as if your body has disappeared. You will almost stop breathing. You will find, when you do Transmission correctly, that there are long periods when you do not seem to breathe. The breathing is so slight, so imperceptible, just enough to keep the body going. Then suddenly, involuntarily, you take a big breath of air.

People indulge in all manner of distractions in Transmission, which they think do not matter. They do, unless you have constant, unbroken alignment between your soul and physical brain. You would not then have to sit still, focused, paying tremendous attention. It would be automatic. Until you have that, it matters. You must take it seriously. You must pay attention and concentrate. If you do not concentrate, you cannot pay attention. If you do not pay attention, you will be unaware of what is happening, except that you are uncomfortable.

The thing is to learn to concentrate, to become aware, to achieve that focus of attention which becomes automatic and takes place whether or not you are making any effort at all, or are comfortable or not.

Is it a good idea to interrupt a Transmission, to walk around to try to help the alignment, and then continue?

People cannot keep aligned for long when they are sitting still trying to keep aligned. Do you think if they get up, walk around, have a drink, a little chat, write a word to their friends, do a few handstands, that somehow that will help their alignment? If you interrupt your concentration and attention that much, is it likely that it will help you to align better? Of course not.

Is it OK during Transmission Meditation to use visualization or the creative imagination in attempts at keeping one's attention at the ajna centre — for example, imagining a light at the centre, or something else?

It is OK to do this but it should not be necessary, and too much effort to do so might well interfere with the alignment between brain and soul which must be maintained.

During Transmission Meditation, is it helpful, or even appropriate, to visualize connecting the ajna chakra with the crown chakra?

No. It is interesting how people dislike simplicity, and always try to make simple methods complicated. Transmission Meditation has been formulated by a Master who, I think, has to be trusted to know best how it should be performed. Please — keep it simple, as presented, without visualization.

You have said you can still feel a sensation in the ajna centre even though your attention has dropped. It is sort of an after-feeling. The question is, how do you differentiate between the two, and how long can that after-feeling go on and can you still be transmitting?

Where are your eyes looking? Your eyes will either be looking through the chakra, in which case you are aligned there, or they will not. There is a kind of negativity which comes in when you focus on the solar plexus. Now I am focusing on the solar plexus, but I am doing it from the ajna. Just watch what is happening. Now I am deliberately experiencing the solar plexus, but you will see that I am doing it from the ajna. It is a conscious intent.

That is different from literally dropping the attention to the solar plexus. You can do anything you like from the ajna centre, if you are focused here. But I am talking about literally dropping the attention and settling into an astral negativity. You can tell if you are focused at the ajna or solar plexus centre. It is a feeling. You can just feel it. Your sensation is in one or the other.

At the Self-Realization Fellowship, they have a picture of Babaji. His eyes are upward almost to the point that they disappear. Is he doing the same thing that we are being asked to do?

If you met Babaji, his eyes would not be up there. He would look normally at you and say: "How do you do?" That is just how He is seen in meditation. His attention is up here, at the top of the head.

Anyone who meditates on the head chakra, the crown, has to turn their eyes upward. But when you do Transmission Meditation, you put your attention on the ajna centre, between the eyebrows. It is not very high up. And you can learn to just hold it there indefinitely. Or you can turn it even higher, but you do not need to do that.

One year I tried literally to look up inwardly with my eyes, and it really had a bad consequence with my physical eyes. It could be a bad thing to do in my case, putting the thinking there...

Yes. The thinking is the important thing, not the turning up of the eyes. All you need to do is hold the attention up. That should not be a strain. If you do it in a rigid way, the eyeballs hurt. But if you do it in a relaxed manner, they pull themselves up and it is held. I think you must have been very rigid.

Is it OK to meditate with your eyes open?

I personally do not recommend it. It is difficult enough to meditate with your eyes shut, without trying to do it with your eyes open. With your eyes open, you are taking in all the experiences that come in through the eyes — all the sensations of light, movement, people, grass, whatever is around you. Meditation is the turning in from that. It is turning towards the soul. If you can shut out all the environment, first of all, it makes the contact with the soul that much easier. That is why you shut your eyes.

Muktananda talked about seeing a blue pearl at the ajna centre when you are aligned. The Sufis talk about seeing a black light.

It is not necessary. You can add all sorts of possibilities. Many teachers have, from their teacher, traditions to make it easier. But you do not have to see anything to hold your attention here. It is simply a turning up of the attention. You do not have to visualize the chakra. You can if you wish. You can visualize a crystal ball, a black light, a pearl, or whatever. This is only a help to visualize the chakra. But in Transmission Meditation, all the work is done for you. We are not invoking the soul. The work is being done by the Masters, who are pouring the energy through the chakra. All you have to do is hold the attention to allow them to do it. You do not even have to visualize the chakra or anything in the chakra. These are two different functions. They are not doing Transmission Meditation. They are teaching their disciples to contact the soul, which is not what we are about. We are using the chakras in the correct way so that the Masters can send Their energies through us. That simply involves the focus — that is all.

HOLDING THE ATTENTION HIGH

It seems that so many of us are so powerfully focused in the solar plexus that we have a difficulty bringing the attention up and holding it at the ajna centre. I am wondering, other than in the meditation, just during the course of the day, doing the things that we do, whether making a conscious effort to work at holding the attention at the ajna centre can help over the long term in being able to hold the attention there?

You have to learn to work from the ajna. Most people work from the solar plexus. It is a question of polarization. If you are under 1.5 to 1.6, you are astrally polarized. That means the seat of your consciousness is the astral plane. This conditions everything you do.

If you are mentally polarized, that will condition the physical reaction. If you tell your body to get on with it and sit still, it will do it. You will forget about it, and it will do its work and sit there; the muscles will hold you upright. But if you fall on the astral nature, which longs for comfort — it is the astral desire that responds to the body's need for comfort, not being in pain or stiff or whatever — then you are in trouble. That is why people cannot sit still. In this country, and it is obviously going to happen in Japan and elsewhere, one of the main killers of this inner stillness, ability to concentrate, is commercial television. The attention span of anyone, from childhood onwards, is minimal. It is cut up into little segments. Whatever they are watching, in a few minutes suddenly comes a commercial. There is a jingle and fast-moving talk, and so on, and their attention is completely shattered. Then after five minutes, they are brought back to the continuation of the story. Then they are engrossed again, their astral nature is satisfied. But this continual shift and change in focus in commercial television is, I think, a great destroyer of concentration. Do not watch commercial television, and keep your attention at the ajna centre at all times.

During Transmission, you are creating the alignment between the brain and the soul by holding the attention at the ajna centre. But when you are going throughout your day, are you creating the same alignment by holding the attention here?

Yes. You are most definitely creating that alignment and maintaining that alignment. That is what the antahkarana is.

If we are only aligned two or three minutes a hour in Transmission, and if people are aligned at different times, do we ever actually have a triangle formed?

You are very pessimistic. You would be surprised. The alignments do synchronize — for a few minutes on and off — enough to make it more than worthwhile to do. This is the point. They are so potent, these energies, that it is the most important thing you could be doing.

Is it almost as valuable to try to do Transmission Meditation alone? Can you actually attract the attention of the Masters? Will it work?

It can. If you use the Great Invocation, the energy will flow. It will not be the same thing, because you do not have the triangle. The triangle potentizes all the energy and is safer; more energy can safely be sent through a group of people who are formed into triangles than through the same number of separate individuals.

During the overshadowing you are focusing on the crown chakra, but my attention seemed to be coming back to my ajna centre because it seemed stronger . . .

No, it just dropped, because it is harder to hold it at the top of the head.

Are there safety considerations for holding the attention at the crown chakra?

Yes, there are. It is safe to hold the attention at the ajna centre. This should eventually become the normal place for your attention. This is the directing centre from which all action is taken. The holding of the attention at the top of the head is only to be done during the overshadowing when I am present. It is not safe for most people to hold their attention at the top of the head. Because they have been doing it when I am here, does not mean they should go on doing it. The ajna centre is the safe centre.

TO "THINK" OM DURING TRANSMISSION

I cannot really understand what it means to "think OM" during Transmission in order to hold my attention on the ajna centre. Do you see the OM?

You do not see the OM, you think OM. It is the thought, the sound of the OM on the mental plane that you use, not seeing it as OM written. It is the sound of the OM, although you are not making a sound. But on the mental plane you are making a sound.

Think OM? Think the sound of OM?

Think OM. Just like you think any thought. Think the OM thought, not written OM, but thought OM.

Maybe the question is, should OM be generalized in your skull or localized at the centre where you want your attention to go?

It should be in the mind, wherever your thought activity is, which will be your brain. You think OM. You say your name is John. Think John. Or Alice. Or Vera. It is a thought like any other thought.

But . . . if we just think the word, like thinking "book" . . .

You do not think it differently, but the word itself is different, that is the point. The OM is the great mantram.

There must be a way of thinking the word where you hear the sound in a better way than we're doing . . .

You do not hear it, you think it. Hearing and thinking are two different things. You can do it fast or slow, but it is thought; it is not different from any other thought, except in its reverberation in the mind. That is what brings your attention to the ajna centre. It is the vibration. If you say "OM" aloud, that vibrates at a certain level. If you say it under your breath (silently), at another. If you think it, that is the highest.

Does the ability to tune into the inner sound inside one's head, the inner OM, have anything to do with overshadowing?

No.

(1) During Transmission Meditation, when one is concentrating on the ajna centre, is it good to breathe at a certain rhythm? (2) By doing so, can you concentrate better?

(1) During Transmission Meditation it is best not to try to regulate or even be aware of the breathing at all. In practice, if the attention is truly held at the ajna centre, it will be found that

the breathing practically stops for quite long periods and restarts with a sudden gasp. It should, in any case, be light, high in the chest, and silent. Do not do breathing exercises. (2) No, you are simply concentrating on the breathing.

How do you reconcile the OM and the breath?

You do not use the OM in relation to the breath at all. You simply think OM. You can think OM any time, whether you are breathing or not breathing. It is not a question of "with the outbreath" or "with the inbreath"; it is simply when you realize that your attention is no longer at the ajna centre that you think OM. The reverberation on the mental plane of the OM brings your attention back to the ajna centre.

Do you send out the OM?

You do not send it out. You think it. It is much simpler than people imagine. You should not do any breathing exercise at all. You simply let the breath follow its own rhythm, and it will get slower and slower until it almost disappears. As it slows, you will find your thoughts slow down. When you are really focused, when your breath is still — just the minimum to keep the body going — there is no thought. You go beyond thought.

BREATH AND THOUGHT

When the breathing slows there is suddenly a feeling of panic, of slight suffocation . . .

If your breathing slows down so much, there will come a point when you will have to take a breath. But there should be no panic. Do not be afraid. Just take a breath. It is easy! You do not have to remind yourself. The slowing down is instinctual, you do not govern that, nor do you govern when you take a breath; your body will tell you. It has its own intelligence. It knows when it needs some oxygen, and then it will take a breath. Forget about the breathing.

Does your breath slow because your focus is going away from breathing to this focus that you are holding?

As you focus on the ajna centre your mental activity slows down. It can speed up, I know. But if you do it correctly you will find fewer and fewer thoughts arising in the mind. As the thoughts slow down, the breathing slows down, and vice versa.

That is why one of the main yogic exercises in controlling thought is to control the breath, because thought and breath come from the same source. If you really focus on the ajna centre and hold it there with the OM for long periods, you find there will be no thought, and therefore no breath. Then you will take a breath and start thinking. You sound the OM again and the whole process repeats.

What source do thought and breath come from?

Find that source. Watch the thought of "I". With every thought that arises in the mind, ask yourself: "Who thought that?" You will say: "I thought it." Take it back: "Who am I?" Trace this sense of "I" and you will find that as you do this, as you go back and back to the source of "I", your thoughts will slow and also the breath. You will find that both are coming from the same source. Experience for yourself where they come from.

Is this related to what Maitreya says: When there is a space between the breathing and thinking, "There I am"?

Yes. That is why He can make use of that space. The point is that what we call breath is the pulse of the universe. The whole of creation is breathing, and we are not separate from that. Our breath is the breath, at this level, of that great pulsation which created all that we can see. That great outbreathing created the universe, all creation. There was not anything, and then there was everything. Then there is the inbreathing, in which all

155

returns to its source. You have the outward movement of creation, and the return movement, involution and evolution. Our breath is intimately related to that breath.

What I am talking about is finding the source of the breath, the source of the "I" thought, the primal thought. Before the "I" thought, you are. But as soon as you think "I", you separate yourself from who you are. Find out who you are, who has the "I" thought. Who is thinking this "I"?

Get the sense of that as the Self, and you will find that what we call breathing, this activity that connects us with the universe, and the thought of "I", come from the same source. There is creation. You are either that, or that which is bringing it into manifestation. Go beyond the "I" thought. Go beyond the breathing and you will find yourself as the Self, which is beyond creation — that which caused breath in the first place, that which breathed out. When you stop the outbreathing and the inbreathing, there is only cause. You are that cause. Experience it.

TRANSMISSION MEDITATION AND REAPPEARANCE WORK

Is Transmission Meditation a priority in the reappearance work?

It is a priority, but not the only priority. The value of Transmission Meditation is that it provides disciples with a field of service second to none in its impact in the world. At the same time, it provides a well, a great reservoir of energy and power from which you can draw at any time. That sustains you. In my experience, the best, the most active, groups, the most effective, have a good, strong Transmission Meditation activity at their base. At the same time, as a field of service, it burns up much of the burden of karma which holds people back. The main hindrance to evolution is karma. Anything which takes the weight of karma from your back should be welcomed, however difficult it is. Obstacles are (karmic) opportunities to overcome and rid yourself of the weight of karma, to resolve it and move forward quickly. Transmission Meditation is the priority in the work of the Transmission Meditation groups. But the first priority is the reappearance work, making known the fact of the reappearance.

People often ask me how far we should go in diluting our work for the reappearance by joining with other groups, doing other kinds of work, getting involved in feeding the hungry, and so on. There are a great many groups serving the cause of hunger, many groups concerned with poverty, many powerful, and more or less effective, agencies at work world-wide.

However, no one in the world except this group is engaged in the work of announcing Maitreya's presence — believing that He is in the world and acting towards that end. There are many groups doing Hierarchical work, who do not believe for a moment that Hierarchy is being externalized and that the Christ is in the world. They work in a different way, subjectively, with less intensity perhaps, and less in response to what is actually happening now. They are doing a more academic type of esoteric work, disseminating information, talking about the various so-called esoteric schools.

They all stem from the same Hierarchical source. They all receive, more or less, Hierarchical energy. The differences in their expression are simply the differences in personality emphasis or ray expression. But we are the only group who, in a very conscious way, is deliberately making known the fact of the Christ's presence in the world.

Other groups — and there are many in all fields (political, economic, social, religious, and so on) — are doing the work of preparation. They do not call it that, because they do not know that is what it is. They are doing this work in an unconscious way — preparing the world, making the changes which make it possible for the Hierarchy to emerge.

How far should you engage in other work? That is up to you. If you take my advice, do not dilute your time and energy too much. You cannot do everything. You cannot change the world individually or as a group, and certainly not overnight. Do what you know to do, which is the work of the reappearance.

That is why you are here. If this group were formed simply to talk about the starving millions, to work with Oxfam or whatever — well, there are marvellous things you could do in many different lines of service now being tackled by many people. But tell me where else there is a group doing what we are doing. That being so, it is common sense to give this work of the reappearance your major time, energy, and effort.

I think there was no need for you to announce the idea of the Day of Declaration because, for those who do Transmission Meditation, Maitreya's emergence does not have much importance. Our purpose should be simply to continue and spread selfless service as transmitters of light to humanity. The announcement of the idea of Declaration instills a sense of expectation in the mind of the transmitter and can lead to the danger of expecting Maitreya unconsciously. Then the work of Transmission, which should be selfless service, will become not for humanity but for oneself and could destroy the purity of the Transmission. (2) Or was this (announcement) done to test transmitters?

I am afraid the questioner has totally misunderstood the purpose behind my work of announcing Maitreya's presence and emergence, and the relation of Transmission Meditation to that event and after.

It is precisely to create the sense of expectation on the widest possible scale that I lecture and write. Far from being a danger to transmitters, this expectation, the more conscious the better, should provide a powerful launching-pad for service, Transmission Meditation, and/or other forms. My task is to inform everyone who will listen, not only those doing Transmission Meditation, about the Day of Declaration, and I really do not see how this information interferes with anyone's selfless service to humanity. Those doing Transmission

Meditation should not see themselves as an elite group somehow separate from humanity as a whole. I believe that everyone needs Maitreya's guidance and teaching, that His emergence is important to us all. Nothing can destroy the purity of the Transmission except the emotional glamours and separative tendencies of those taking part. (2) It goes without saying that my announcement of Maitreya's emergence is done with total seriousness of purpose and not to test anyone at all.

After the Day of Declaration, what will be the practical benefit of Transmission Meditation work in the short term?

Transmission Meditation is not simply a way of distributing energies to bring about the Declaration of the Christ. It is a long-term process by which Hierarchical energies can be made available to the mass of humanity at a level that can be absorbed and used. It is also a process which will bring those involved in its practice to the Gates of Initiation. It is a way of co-operating with the Masters of the Hierarchy in serving the world and, at the same time, a yoga of self-development of enormous practical benefit to those taking part in it.

CHAPTER X

THE ROLE OF TRANSMISSION MEDITATION IN THE DEVELOPMENT OF THE DISCIPLE — ITS UNDERLYING PURPOSE

The following article is an edited transcription of talks given by Creme at the Transmission Meditation conferences held in the United States and Holland in 1987. The conferences were attended by regular members of Transmission Meditation groups in North America and Europe. The relevant questions and answers raised during the conferences are also included.

The work of Transmission Meditation has spread throughout the world, and the number of people who join or start Transmission groups is increasing all the time. It is interesting to note that the information contained in the following article is given by Benjamin Creme's Master at this time. It is, perhaps, a good example of the way that Hierarchy imparts more and more teaching and information to disciples as their development and capacities allow.

UP UNTIL NOW, when I have talked or written about Transmission Meditation, I have, on the whole, emphasized its service aspect. If Transmission Meditation is anything at all, it is undoubtedly an act of service to the world.

But there is even more than service to Transmission Meditation. It is not possible to have these great spiritual forces transmitted through the group without these individuals becoming transformed. As the energies pass through the chakras, they stimulate and heighten the activity of the various chakras, above all the heart, the throat and the head. Because of this, Transmission Meditation is probably the most useful method of personal growth open to any individual today. It is like a hot-house, a forcing process; therefore, it is not for everybody. But for those who are ready for this stimulus it is, par excellence, the method of fast evolution. In one year of sustained and correct Transmission Meditation, a person can make the same evolutionary advance as in 10 to 15 years of ordinary meditation. It is therefore an enormous stimulus to the evolutionary process.

Up until now, most meditations have been given, at least in the beginning, to specific groups who could handle the meditation, perform its rigorous rules and requirements, and then gradually release it more exoterically into the world. These have taken their place as the various forms of meditation which are habitually used throughout the world. Each of them is a technique which brings one into contact with one's soul. That is what meditation is about. The Masters, up until now, have been concerned with bringing the more advanced units of humanity to a point where they can make contact with their souls and build the antahkarana, the channel of light between the man or woman in incarnation and the individual's soul.

An entirely new process is now under way. A new energy is entering our world, the 7th ray of Ceremonial Order, Ritual, or Organization, as well as the incoming energies of Aquarius which work towards synthesis. The Aquarian energies can be sensed, apprehended, and utilized only in group formation.

Until now, most of the emphasis in development has been on the individual disciple. This has been necessitated by the individualizing quality of the 6th ray of Devotion, or Idealism, which has dominated our world over the last 2,000-plus years. This ray is now going out of incarnation, and we are being influenced more and more by the 7th ray, which stimulates group activity because of its organizing quality, as do the Aquarian energies as they impinge on our lives.

Another great factor is the externalization of the Spiritual Hierarchy who, for millennia, have remained out of sight, occult, in Their retreats in the mountains and deserts of the world. They are returning to the world now in quite substantial numbers. My information is that there are now 12 Masters in the world and Their numbers will gradually increase until there are, over the next 20 years or so, around 40 Masters working openly in the world. [*Editor's note*: 14 Masters as of 1997.]

This highly unusual occurrence brings altogether more potent energies into our lives and opens up entirely new possibilities for humanity. Particularly is this so for the disciples and aspirants of the world and for Hierarchy in its long-term plan of fusing the centre, Hierarchy, where the Love of God is expressed, and the centre, humanity, where the Intelligence of God demonstrates.

This will lead eventually to a fusion of all three major centres, including Shamballa, "the centre where the Will of God is known". For the present, however, over the next 2,500 year period, the Masters of the Hierarchy will work towards the gradual fusion of Their centre and that of humanity.

The major work of the Christ, as the World Teacher for this coming cycle, is to bring humanity into the Spiritual Hierarchy, through the first two doors, the first and second initiations. This is a long term plan, and steps for bringing this about are to some extent underway.

As far as the disciples are concerned, the Masters work as potently, as specifically, as the disciples themselves allow. No information, no form or technique is withheld which can be safely applied or known. We ourselves condition the degree to which the teaching and the techniques necessary for the immediate future development can be given.

Transmission Meditation is one of the major forms for bringing about an alignment between the two kingdoms, the Kingdom of God, the Spiritual Hierarchy, and the human kingdom. This is because it is a technique which links the activity of these two groups. Transmission Meditation is the means by which Hierarchy releases its energy through groups and which, at the same time, by the karmic adjustments thus made, enables Them to work with these groups in a way far closer than would otherwise be possible.

The Masters, up until now, have worked with groups only insofar as the groups can respond to Their impression. Groups work from self or soul-initiated work, from Hierarchical impression, or from direct Hierarchical supervision. The senior disciples work under direct supervision, and many of them work through groups who respond from their own soul influence, or from the rather more remote influence of the Masters.

The Masters are anxious to develop a closer rapport, a working relationship, with the disciples of the world. As They emerge, Their hope is that They will not remain too far distant from the working disciples and will be able to work in the closest conscious co-operation with them. Of course it will take time to develop that close relationship. Transmission Meditation has been given as a starting point for this to take place. It brings a man or woman from simple relation to their own soul, to the creation, through group Transmission, of a *group soul* through which the Master can work.

Transmission Meditation is the method par excellence for groups to form their own group soul. It is not something that one sets about doing consciously, but which happens from the interrelated activity of the individuals in the group.

Transmission Meditation, because it takes place from the soul level, gradually provides the field in which the group soul can be synthesized. The group soul is not the sum total of the individual rays of a group, however many involved, but a synthesis of the forces which make up that group. The group can be made up of people on various soul rays, with a variety of personality, mental, astral, and physical rays. From the synthesis formed by Transmission Meditation is evolved a new, distinctive note, which the Master can stimulate and work through. This relates the group to a Master, not simply on an individual basis but in a group sense. The Masters send the energies through the group with two purposes always in mind. Firstly, the service of distribution of Their energies, and secondly (and for Them just as importantly), the gradual transformation of the qualities of the individuals in the group into a blended soul ray, with a specific purpose given to it by the soul of the group. In this way, the group becomes a potent outpost for the work of the Spiritual Hierarchy. They can use such a group by stimulation and impression to do certain work which any individual Master may have as a part of His specific area of the Plan.

The general Plan of evolution comes from Shamballa. Brought by the Buddha to Hierarchy, it is outlined by the Christ, the Manu, and the Mahachohan. Each Master takes a portion of the Plan which He knows intuitively will suit His own abilities, and He seeks to develop through His groups the working out of His particular aspect of the Plan.

This is not a one-way process. The work of the groups themselves often stimulates a development of the Master's Plan. I know, for instance, that my Master is doing work which He never planned to do, answering questions, writing books, and giving ray structures of initiates with their points of evolution. However, groups around the world have evoked from me responses which have, in turn, brought responses from the Master, and these have developed and conditioned the work which the Master has done. This is an extraordinary happening. This is the way the Masters want to work. They seem to have unending time, energy, and enthusiasm for what must be for Them very tedious tasks.

I remember when the rays were being assembled for *Share International*. I had 578, not a memorable number at all, and I had a list of more to do, some of them pretty high initiates, I felt. It was coming up to publishing time and I was hoping I would get 600, as that would be a good round number. The Master one day said to me, quite suddenly:"You know, it's so good of you to provide me with this field of service. It is so boring up here, sitting twiddling my thumbs, with nothing to do. I'm so grateful to you for giving me these rays to look up. I'm so happy about this." I smelled a rat. He continued: "Do not ask for another ray structure of any kind until I give the word, which will be several months from now." I said: "But we've only got 578 and I would like all these others." He said firmly: "No, no more. In a few months you may." I said: "Well, we've got this third-degree

initiate, and that one could be a fourth — really advanced ones."
I pleaded: "I would like a nice round figure, please?" Finally He
consented and said: "All right, that one and that one and that's
the lot." So there were 580.

[*Editor's note*: This list of initiates has been reprinted, together
with 40 additional names, as an appendix to *Maitreya's Mission*,
Vol. I, by Benjamin Creme. A further list of 201 names appears
as an appendix to *Maitreya's Mission*, Vol. II. *Maitreya's
Mission*, Vol. III, contains the complete list of 950 names.]

He is so kind, so generous with His time that the work gets
done, and in this way He has given to the world information
never given before, which to the student is absolutely
fascinating. If one looks at the point in evolution of people like
Mahatma and Indira Gandhi, Hitler, Julius Caesar, or whomever,
it puts one's own ideas about evolution in perspective. It is
extremely interesting and I know that a great many people have
found it of enormous benefit.

This is the way in which groups themselves can evoke from
a Master work which He did not anticipate doing. Of course, if a
Master does not intend to do something, He will not do it unless
He sees some worthwhile purpose in doing it.

Transmission Meditation has been given to provide us with
a field of development, and to provide Hierarchy itself with a
field of expression through which They can work and bring
together the human kingdom and the Spiritual Kingdom. Its
underlying purpose is to bring the groups involved through the
portals of initiation. Through initiation, the two kingdoms are
merged, and, as already stated, the major aim of the Christ in
this age is to bring humanity into the Spiritual Kingdom.

The reason that the Masters, after thousands of years, can
come back into the world is because humanity is now ready to
enter the Kingdom of God, the Spiritual Kingdom. After 18-and-
a-half million years, humanity is ready to take that step and to
become the world disciple. At long last humanity is coming of
age and achieving that first step into divinity. This is an

extraordinary event in the development of humanity and is behind the externalization of Hierarchy.

The Master D.K. wrote (through Alice A. Bailey) about a specialized form of Laya Yoga which will be the yoga of the new age. Laya Yoga is the yoga of energies, of the centres. This specialized form of Laya Yoga is indeed already known. It is called Transmission Meditation.

Transmission Meditation is a fusion of two yogas: Laya Yoga, the yoga of energies, and Karma Yoga, the yoga of service. It combines precisely these two most potent forms of evolution. Nothing moves a man or woman so quickly along the path of evolution than being engaged powerfully, potently, in some form of service. That is Karma Yoga. It is the lever of the evolutionary process.

The other equally important leverage is meditation. Meditation brings one into contact with one's soul and eventually into contact with the Kingdom of Souls. The combination of these two, service and meditation, is the most potent method of pushing one along the path of evolution, taking one on to the path of discipleship, to the path of initiation and eventually to Mastery.

The Masters call Their work the Great Service. They are here only to serve. They have made that Their work, Their reason for being, because They know that there is nothing more important in the whole of the manifested universe than service.

That there is a universe at all is due to the service activity of the great Consciousness which stands behind it and has brought it into manifestation. The reason that we are on this planet, as thoughtforms in the mind of the creating Logos, is because the Logos Himself is serving the Plan of evolution of the Solar Logos. We are part of that great Plan and, if the Solar Logos sees service as the be-all and end-all of His activity, then I think, as dim reflections of that deity, we may conclude that we must ourselves be about service. It could not be otherwise. Service takes us back eventually, in full Logoic consciousness, to identity with the Logos of which we are a part.

Meditation and service, linked, provide the means. Transmission Meditation brings together these two most potent levers of the evolutionary process — Laya, the yoga of energies, and Karma, the yoga of service. They impel the people involved in it fast along the last phase of evolution: the path of initiation.

The vast majority of those taking part in Transmission work, as a really important part of their lives, giving time and energy to it, have already taken the first initiation, whether they know it or not. Otherwise, they would not be in a Transmission group. They would not have the desire to serve in this fashion.

Most people entering group work are drawn into an activity where they can see themselves, talk about themselves, learn about themselves. They are concerned with advancing and knowing themselves and developing this faculty and that faculty. 'Channelling' has become the 'in thing' in the New Age groups. Transmission Meditation does not provide the format for all these interesting personality things — it is just sitting doing apparently nothing. Nothing seems to be happening. It is certainly not something about which you can say: "Do you know what happened tonight? I learned who I was in my last life." You cannot go home and say that. Nobody is telling you who you were — Cleopatra or whoever. You are just sitting there allowing these energies to go through you. Some people find this a little difficult to see as valuable.

If you do it, you must be doing it for the service that it gives the world. Therefore, if you do it consistently and thoroughly, you will almost certainly have taken the first initiation. Otherwise, you would not be interested.

Therefore, most have passed through the portals at least once and, as the Christ says in His message No. 21: "I shall take you to Him when you are ready, when you have passed through the Gates twice, and stood shining before Me." That means bring them to the third initiation.

One of the most important duties of the Christ is as "nourisher of the little ones", as it is called. That involves nourishing those who have taken the first two initiations and preparing them for the third.

One is already initiate as one stands before the Initiator; the Christ at the first two initiations and the Lord of the World at the third and higher initiations. Otherwise one's chakras could not stand the inflow of the fire from the rod of initiation: in the case of the first two initiations, of the *Lesser Rod* as it is called, used by the Christ, or, at the third and higher initiations, the *Flaming Diamond,* which is charged from the Central Spiritual Sun and is focused through the chakras of the initiate by the Lord of the World.

One of the major tasks of the Christ is to so stimulate the aspirants and disciples of the world that they can pass through the 'Gates' twice before Him — take the first two initiations — and come before the Lord of the World Himself, take the third initiation, and become divine.

The Masters think of initiation and to be initiate as having taken the third initiation. The first two are really preparatory, integrating the personality, with its physical, astral, and mental bodies, into a whole. When that takes place, the third initiation becomes possible. So the task of the Christ is to nourish what appear to be individuals but what are in reality groups, because behind every individual is a group. We see the individuals; the Masters see the groups.

Since They are coming into the world now, They are stimulating the formation of groups who actually see each other, work together, and create from their activity a group soul, vibrating at a particular rate. The vibration which the group soul itself generates through Transmission Meditation and service (which Transmission Meditation is) can then be stimulated and utilized by the Masters and eventually by Maitreya Himself.

The "nourishing of the little ones" takes place on two levels. Those who have already taken the second initiation are stimulated directly by Maitreya. Those between the first and second initiation are also nourished, today, by the process of overshadowing. As I go from group to group and He

169

overshadows me, it becomes a group overshadowing, and in this way Maitreya is able to do for them what He could not otherwise do. The energy is 'stepped down' to a point where it can safely do the nourishing work. It is an experiment which He has undertaken since He is overshadowing me anyway.

Everything the Masters do produces many offshoots of that same activity and so the work generates more activity and a greater expression of Their purpose.

The underlying purpose, then, of Transmission Meditation is to provide the means, the stimulus, to bring the groups involved in it to the portal of initiation. First of all, there is the energetic stimulus of the energies passing through the chakras. As people take part in the Transmission work, their chakras are stimulated altogether more potently than would otherwise be the case. We ourselves condition the degree to which the stimulus takes place. By our service, our activity, we gradually develop a dynamism in the chakras, which allows the Masters to give more. "To them who have shall be given." This does not mean that if you are rich you will get more money. It means that if your chakras are open, vibrating, and radiant, you can actually receive more energy, because you magnetically draw it and it can safely be given. So as you take part in Transmission Meditation, you provide the Masters and yourself with a field of work in which the stimulus is exactly, scientifically, proportionate to your ability to serve. They provide the energy and, as you put that into use, you magnetically draw more energy to you with every Transmission in which you take part. It has to be continuous, of course. It is a dynamic process and has to be done consistently and regularly.

With every Transmission, you gradually develop an ability to receive higher potencies of the energies and expand your sensitivity to different energies.

One of the great experiments going on in Hierarchy at the moment is the relating of the various ashrams. There are three major departments: that of the Manu, the Christ, and the Mahachohan, and then the various ashrams of the subsidiary rays. The problem for Hierarchy has always been to find groups who can work in a sophisticated way. For instance, although the Master Morya is on the 1st ray and the Master Koot Hoomi is on the 2nd ray, They always work together. They have done so for centuries, and I have no doubt They will go on doing so for the next 2,500 years, because of the close relationship between the 1st and 2nd ray. So the Masters of Love and the Masters of Will work together in the closest association and harmony, with an identity of purpose, and methods of work, which, although different, interact and correspond to the inner need as They envision that need.

In the outer field, among the disciples, They seek to bring about that same state of affairs. The Hierarchy is a totality of seven major ashrams, each with six subsidiary ashrams, making 49 altogether. The eventual aim is that these 49 ashrams should be working together in the closest harmony and relationship to each other; an interaction working out in such a way that each contributes its own definite ray method to the Plan in relation to all the others, not separately but together.

They foresee a time in which we ourselves will work in that kind of interrelationship. So there is an experiment going on in Hierarchy in which the Transmission groups, on whatever ray they may be, are given opportunities to work with rays other than their own.

I do not know if it is true for groups who do not do Transmission Meditation, but in the groups with which I work this experiment has been going on since March 1974, when the first Transmission Meditation group was formed in London at the behest of my Master.

At some time in the course of the Transmission, each group is given the opportunity to work with, to have transmitted through them, rays which may be quite foreign to their ray structures. Ray structures vary (a group might contain more or less all the rays), but most groups tend to be, by gravitational attraction, on the same soul ray. I have found that the rays of countries seem to determine the dominant ray of the groups to be found in those countries. It is not by chance, nor is it haphazard.

In this work, groups are drawn from all the rays because of the particular synthesizing, attractive force of this message of the reappearance of the Christ and the Masters of Wisdom. The groups with which I work are those who have responded to that message in some way or other. It tends to draw people whose ray structures allow them, more easily than others, to be attracted to the work. There are not too many people, for instance, who would, in the normal course of affairs, be in politics or economics or science. They tend to be from the metaphysical groups, or are people who have a 2nd-ray interest in some of the metaphysical disciplines. What draws people to this work is the fact that the message about the reappearance of the Christ has caught their imagination. Their soul has responded. Their intuition tells them this is true or may be true and so they have gravitated to the work. That brings them into contact with energies which they then utilize in various ways.

Most people in the Transmission groups are somewhere between the first and second initiation and are getting ready to come before the Christ and take the second initiation, the baptism. This is the outcome of mental polarization. The second initiation becomes possible when the astral elemental is sufficiently dominated from the mental level, through mental polarization, so as to weaken its hold on the individual's astral nature. By our emotional activity we draw energy from the astral plane through our powerful astral body, developed over some 12 million years of the Atlantean root race and now so powerful it dominates most of humanity. Through its extraordinary potency, it keeps humanity in thrall to its emotional nature, and eventually it has to be controlled. It is created out of the life activity of tiny astral elementals, just as our physical body is created from the activity of the physical elementals. These are tiny devic lives who make up our bodies, physical, astral, and mental. These are matter. Even our mental body is made of matter of the mental plane. That matter is created by the elementals of the plane. They dominate us or we dominate them. Eventually, of course, by the sheer pressure of evolution, by the pull of the great cosmic magnet which sweeps the whole evolutionary cycle into being, we are brought to the point where we have to face this problem: dominating first the physical elemental and taking the first initiation, then the astral elemental and taking the second initiation.

Transmission Meditation is literally a gift from the gods. It speeds up the process enabling us in no time at all, compared with previous cycles, to dominate the astral vehicle. There is nothing more potent in bringing about the domination of that vehicle than Transmission Meditation. Because of the scientific method by which the Masters work, it produces the conditions in which mental polarization becomes possible.

Mental polarization starts half-way between the first and second initiation. The average number of lives between the first and second initiation is about six to seven, and most of that time is taken going from 1 to 1.5. So anyone who knows that they are around 1.5 should realize that if they are young enough they can probably take the second initiation in this life. As soon as mental polarization is reached, the whole process speeds up tremendously.

There is a very important plan which relates to the groups involved in Transmission Meditation. They will see the Christ far sooner than they think possible. I do not mean in the sense of His coming out before the world — that is happening anyway — but in a much more personal way. Those engaged in Transmission Meditation who are now around 1.4 or 1.5 will almost certainly come before the Christ *in this life* and take the second initiation. Transmission Meditation has been given at this time to enable this to take place and to provide the Christ and the Masters with very potent groups, already formed all over the world, who can act as stimulants to the rest and so speed up the whole process of evolution.

The Master D.K. has said that the most important thing you can do for the world is to control the astral vehicle and become mentally polarized. You free the ethers of the world from the impact of your astral, emotional activity which so discolours them. The plan, the underlying purpose, is to bring as many groups as quickly as possible before the Christ at the second initiation, so a large group of prepared people in the Transmission groups will come before Maitreya and receive the initiating energy from the rod.

That is why the Christ acts so powerfully in this overshadowing process to nourish the groups. He is doing it now, experimentally, through me to bring Transmission groups all over the world to the point where they can stand before Him and become really potent, active workers. One has to have taken the second initiation to be really active in a way that can be trusted by Hierarchy: to work intelligently, objectively, without the interference of astral glamour. To do good objective work for the Plan, one needs to be at or close to the second initiation.

They wish everybody to get through that hurdle, because it is enormous. The second initiation is the most difficult of all the initiations to take. That is why so much help is needed to get over this hurdle.

I am told to present to you this promise and opportunity: Initiation in this life. Go to it!

[*Editor's note:* For further information on the rays and initiations, see *Maitreya's Mission,* Vols. I and II, by Benjamin Creme.]

Could you describe the evolutionary process from the point of view of the disciple, particularly the stages between first and second initiation?

The disciple is someone who is *consciously* taking part in the evolutionary journey. It goes without saying that all of humanity is evolving; has evolved from early animal man to the point where we are today. For untold aeons of time, that process has taken place more or less unconsciously. The individual soul comes into incarnation again and again, swept into evolution by the magnet of evolution itself.

The disciple, on the other hand, takes a very conscious role in this process, leading to a very specific goal. The mass of humanity do not really know that there is an end point, a goal, at least as it relates to this planet.

The disciple is someone who knows there is a goal, and seeks to further his evolution himself in a highly conscious manner. The goal he sees is, of course, perfection — liberation from the necessity to incarnate on the planet at all. The disciple willingly and consciously submits himself to the necessary discipline — that is what being a disciple is — to arrive finally at that goal.

There are five great points of crisis which mark out the evolutionary process. These are the five initiations to Mastery or Liberation. After that you do not need to incarnate on this planet. These five great expansions of consciousness, which is what initiation is, cover only the last few lives of the evolutionary journey from animal man to the totally liberated Master. It takes literally hundreds of thousands of incarnational experiences before the person can be prepared for the first initiation. As the soul sees its vehicle coming close to that point, perhaps four or five incarnations yet away from the first initiation, it brings its vehicle, the man or woman on the physical plane, into contact with some form of meditation.

In that first instance, it may be very slight indeed; the person hears about meditation, tries it for a bit, perhaps spends a little part of his time doing it. Eventually comes a life in which the person will spend a considerable part of his time devoted to the practice of some form of meditation. It is not the personality who seeks meditation; it is forced into this process by the impulse of the soul itself. In this sense the soul is the first Master.

When, through several lives passed in a more serious approach to meditation, the person becomes ready for the first initiation, the Master steps in and guides, tests, and prepares the person for this extraordinary first expansion of consciousness.

In incarnation are roughly 800,000 people who have taken the first initiation. (Of course, there are many out of incarnation who have also gone through this experience.) Out of five billion people, it is not very many. Of those who have taken the second initiation, there are only some 240,000 in incarnation; of the third, only between 2,000 and 3,000. Of those who have taken the fourth initiation, there are only about 450 in the world at the moment. The numbers are very small indeed. The interesting thing today is that the process is speeding up extraordinarily. Now, several million people are standing at the threshold of the first initiation. That is why the Hierarchy, for the first time in countless thousands of years, are returning to the everyday world — the disciples are drawing Them back magnetically.

The probationary disciple is watched and tested by a Master, at the fringe of the Master's Ashram. When he has passed his tests and is ready, he enters through the gate of initiation into Hierarchy and becomes a disciple. That is the beginning of a journey from which there is no return, the burning of the boats behind the disciple. He can waste many lives, hold himself back, but he really cannot ever turn back against the tide of evolution.

Then he enters a period where a great battle is fought out between his soul and his personality. The man or woman on the physical plane becomes the arena of battle for possession between his personality desire life and the spiritual life of the soul. Eventually, though it may take some time, the soul, because it is stronger, wins.

The battle can rage for many lives. There is an average of six or seven lives between the first and second initiation. It is a very hard struggle, and a painful one, in the beginning, for the disciple. He finds that he is being stimulated on all fronts — mentally, emotionally, and physically. His three bodies are stimulated as never before. The battle has to be fought out simultaneously on all three fronts. As he thinks he is coping with the enemy attacking his physical frontier, he finds himself invaded on the emotional front. He brings all his personality forces to bear to thrust the enemy back, and he finds that on the mental plane and on the physical plane, again, there are forces attacking him from behind. Eventually, by the sheer exhaustion of the battle, he gives in.

He becomes an accepted disciple under the supervision and discipline of a Master, working closer to the centre of a Master's Ashram. Then he discovers that he is not alone, and never has been alone, as he thought, but that he is really part of a group, the members of which he has probably never met on the physical plane. He works under the supervision, not immediately of a Master, but of a disciple of one of the Masters. He finds that the battle rages more and more fiercely until he comes to a point about half way between the first and second initiation.

Suddenly he sees a little glimmer of light at the end of a long tunnel. He finds that the physical body is obeying his will, and that the most unruly body of all, his astral body, (at least, two or three times out of 100!) begins to be controlled. He finds this very encouraging — he sees a way ahead. It is still a fight, but he sees that, if he keeps at it, there is hope.

Then he finds that he is put in contact with other people in some group work. He finds that these other people have exactly the same experiences, the same difficulties, and he realizes that this is part of growing out of his ignorance, glamour, illusion, and beginning to see the world and reality and himself as they really are.

To bring all of this about, meditation has been given to the world. It is the catalytic process which allows the soul to create this situation vis-à-vis its reflection. It grips its vehicle, mentally, astrally, physically, more and more, making it a purer reflection of itself. Its aim is to bring its vehicle into a perfect reflection of itself. It does this by stimulating the vibrational rate of each of the bodies, physical, astral and mental, until all three are vibrating at more or less the same frequency.

The soul is in no hurry. It has aeons of time, because it does not even think in terms of time. It is only the man or woman, the personality, who has the feeling that this is taking forever. It seems to us that we will never be free of these physical, astral, and mental controls which prevent us from expressing ourselves as the soul, the spiritual being, we know we are, whose spiritual intelligence, love, and will is demonstrating and radiant. When that point is eventually reached, the third great expansion of consciousness can be taken.

This is a watershed in the evolutionary process. From the point of view of the Masters, this is the first initiation. The first two are seen by Them as preparatory initiations to this first true soul initiation when the man or woman really becomes ensouled — and therefore truly divine — for the first time. Until then the divinity is there but only in potential.

Two factors bring this about: meditation of some form or other, bringing the man or woman into contact with the soul; the other is service — some form of altruistic service.

Will you explain a bit more about Karma Yoga and Laya Yoga?

Karma Yoga is the yoga of service. Imagine yourself going through this incarnation with a great load of karma on your shoulders, or dragging it behind you in a huge sled over very rough ground. You pull and pull, but it gets stuck in every little rut. The deeds and misdeeds of your past are all carried along with you, not just from your past lives, but yesterday's, last week's, last year's, and when you were a child.

All of that is our karma. All that we have ever set in motion, every effect of every cause makes our karma. That has to be resolved, the karmic knots have to be untied, so that we can go on and become Masters with no personal karma at all. That is the aim of the evolutionary process.

In terms of Karma Yoga, the Law of Karma becomes the Law of Service. This Law gives us the opportunity to balance the negative karma built up over many lives. Karma Yoga is the serving of the world as dispassionately, as detachedly as one can. It is as if there is a big scale, on one side of which are piled our past misdeeds — the result of our imperfections — and on the other, our service activity. We have to throw more and more onto that pan through service to gradually balance this weight of karma and resolve it. Service burns up the karma by bringing about the balance of the two. That is Karma Yoga.

Laya Yoga is the yoga of energy of the chakras. This yoga underlies the manipulation of energies of cosmos, but in the sense in which we use it, it is the yoga by which the Masters transmit their energies through the groups. It is a very occult yoga performed for us by the Masters. They are experts, Master Scientists. Every second of every hour, They are transmitting and transforming the energies from some extra-planetary source (protecting humanity from those which would be harmful).

Can you imagine having such advanced scientists overseeing your own meditation? Yet everyone who does Transmission Meditation enters a field of service so simple that a child of 12 can do it, but on the other hand has energies sent through him so scientifically that the fastest advance along the evolutionary path becomes possible. Transmission Meditation is introduced to the world at this time because only now are groups of disciples forming who are able to handle such potent energies, and to work consciously in group formation.

Gradually, we will assist the Masters in manipulating these energies and in this way save Them time and energy.

Now that we know we can take our evolution into our own hands, is this as good for the world — in a spiritual sense — as acting totally altruistically in service for the world?

Yes, I would say so. Whatever you take into your own hands and work consciously at will be more purposeful and better directed than what you do without direction or purpose. Then the stimulus of the Will comes into the process. The Will is necessary to provide the driving, impelling force towards initiation. Service of whatever kind will gradually bring you to the gate of initiation. Laya Yoga, the precise, scientific yogic process which Transmission Meditation is, provides the direction and potency to the service which drives you forward.

One of the questions which often comes up about Transmission Meditation is that people are unaware of the results. They do not see a result from the Transmission and they wonder if in fact they are doing any good for the world. Simply in serving, they have to take it on faith that they are helping the world. They cannot see the result of the Transmission and say, "Such and such an event was due to me. That was because I took part in the wonderful Transmission last night." You cannot expect that kind of cause and effect in Transmission Meditation. But what you can see is the change in yourself. And when you know that in this life you could take the second initiation — and control the astral vehicle — that in itself should impel you to join a Transmission group.

If the energy of love isn't correctly used, how does this demonstrate in the physical body?

If the energy of the soul, whose nature is intelligence, love and will, is not correctly used, this can manifest itself as physical illness, emotional disturbance and/or mental instability. If you do correct meditation — I am not talking about Transmission Meditation alone — and correct service, you will find that all goes normally and rightly. You do not get ill, or if you do, it is a karmic illness, something from the past which you have to deal with. There are two kinds of illness on the path of discipleship: the illness, physical, astral or mental, which is the result of the non-use or misuse of soul energy; and, especially at the end of the path of initiation, illnesses which are simply the ending for the individual of the burden of karma.

For instance, let us take the case of two very well-known initiates, H.P. Blavatsky and Alice A. Bailey, fourth- and third-degree initiates respectively. They were ill for a considerable part of their lives. In the last 12 or so years of Madame Blavatsky's life, she had several illnesses, all at once. But none of these physical illnesses prevented her from doing her work as a major, senior disciple, working with the Masters, and giving an invaluable body of information to the world. Likewise with Alice Bailey. These illnesses were not the result of their misuse of soul energy. On the contrary, no one could have used their soul energy more correctly, more scientifically, more in line with the purpose of their souls, than these two initiates. They were both totally soul-infused individuals. In their case, their illnesses were the paying of karmic debts which would finally rid them of the karma of the past and lead them to the door of liberation.

In lesser disciples, illnesses are largely the result of their non-use or misuse of soul energy. It 'goes bad' on them and they become neurotic. As soon as you make contact with the soul, you contact very powerful forces. If you do not utilize these forces in service they will damage your physical, astral, or mental vehicles. This is the reason for the illnesses — mainly psychological, nervous and astral — of disciples. With correct, scientific meditation, correct use of the energies invoked in service, the physical body, the astral nature, and the mental body can carry out their purposes in the right way, and the health of all three is maintained without any effort on the part of the individual.

The turning point is 1.5, half way between the first and second initiations. The major stress occurs between 1.3 and 1.6. The person becomes aware of the glamours of the astral plane. He realizes that up until now, almost every response he has made to life has been astral, a glamour and unreal. This has been the case all the way to the first initiation. While the person is totally immersed in the glamours, not seeing them at all, there is for him no problem, because the reactions are automatic, astral, emotional responses, which are identified with completely and accepted as real. But around 1.3 to 1.5 or 1.6, he begins to react more from the mental plane because the influence of the soul is getting stronger.

The light of the soul, shining through the mental body at the glamours, begins to show these reactions as unreal. Until this point, the person is quite happy with his glamours, his illusions, his unreal reactions to life. But when you see that your emotional reactions are unreal, that they are not 'you', it is painful, and makes you suffer. The impulse then is to try to do something about these reactions, to get rid of them — and that increases the suffering, the power of the glamour. The more effort we make to get rid of a glamour, the stronger we will make it. We have to learn the art of recognizing or looking at the glamours, and at the unreality of our responses, without trying to change them. Simply by our looking at them and not giving them energy, they will die from lack of nourishment. That process is at its height between 1.3 and 1.6. Of course, the emotional nature is being stimulated all the time by the soul and so it is a very difficult time. Transmission Meditation helps you through this process, because in Transmission Meditation you are gradually shifting the polarization from the astral to the mental plane.

Can you explain how Transmission Meditation helps bring about mental polarization?

It does so by bringing us into a higher state of spiritual tension. In that higher state, by the Transmission work, our chakras are charged by the spiritual energies, and our physical, astral, and mental bodies are stimulated and galvanized. The dross from the astral plane is brought up to the surface and resolved, and we stand in a more or less continuous state of unusual spiritual tension. Of course, this only occurs if we do it regularly and consistently.

When the vehicles are charged, the soul can work through them, galvanizing and 'gripping' them, thus increasing the spiritual tension. Every influx of spiritual energy is an opportunity for the soul to grip its vehicle more firmly. The more the soul does this, the more the individual becomes mentally polarized, because it is through the light of the soul playing through the mental body that the astral body is controlled. The shift to mental polarization takes place as the astral body is gradually controlled. When it is sufficiently controlled, we take the second initiation.

This process of creating and sustaining — sustaining is the important thing — a continuous spiritual tension in life, where the aspiration becomes less and less astral and more and more mental (and eventually spiritual), enables the soul to really work through its vehicles. Then the intuition comes into play, and the light of the soul, through the mind, illumines the whole area of astral glamour and illusion. These are gradually dissipated and controlled until we stand clear enough to take the second initiation.

The process of mental polarization starts at around 1.5, and continues until halfway between the second and third initiation. So mental polarization is not completed until 2.5. Then begins spiritual polarization. The spiritual tension is then so complete that the soul is really the focus of consciousness.

If the average has been six or seven lifetimes between the first and second initiations, once Transmission becomes an ordinary part of our lifestyle what do you think the average time frame will be?

That is impossible to say, but obviously it will drop tremendously. Every disciple who speeds up his evolution contributes to the speed of evolution for the rest. It is always in relation to the spiritual intensity which we bring to bear. The spiritual tension generated in the planet draws the Hierarchy back into the world; that is why They are returning. This specialized form of Laya Yoga, Transmission Meditation, is specifically designed to speed up the evolution of the disciple *because* the Masters are coming into the world. They wield a tremendous force. The spiritual potency of these Men is quite extraordinary. One Master can galvanize the activity of everybody around Him. When we have 40 Masters as well as Maitreya working openly in the world, and a much larger number of fourth-degree initiates (at the moment there are about 450) together with more of every other grade, then we will get a spiritual intensity in the world which will make it possible for people to go from the first initiation to the second in three, two, maybe eventually one life. I do not know if it will be in this age, but certainly the time will be shortened.

How does the formation of a group soul help a group's ability to take the second initiation, or to speed up the process?

By the intensity of its activity, a group sets up a spiritual tension which in due course manifests itself as a group soul. It has a group identity and sounds a certain note. On the physical plane, it is the tone given out by the personality of the group. On the soul level, it is the note given out through the intensity of the spiritual purpose of the group, and that gradually creates, through the relationships between the souls making up the group, a synthesis which is a group soul. It is the synthesis of the soul power of that group.

The group may not all have the same soul ray; nevertheless they form an entity which is called a group soul. That group soul, in relationship to the group on the physical plane, acts rather like your own ashramic group. Every ashram is made up of individuals around a nucleus — a Master — who draws to Himself the various disciples whom He finds He is able to allow near Him (you have to be kept on the periphery for a certain time so that you do not disturb the group work). When you can attain and hold steady a certain vibration, you can be brought closer to the group and closer to the Master, until you can work quite closely with and be really useful to Him. But the most important thing for the disciple to know, consciously, is that he is a member of that soul group and can draw on the energy of the group.

When group souls are created through the Transmission work, they are not forming new ashrams, but they are like a tiny sub-ashram. From, perhaps, different ashrams, souls come together to form another entity. This is related through the individual souls to the various ashrams and may work with several of the rays. The aim today of Hierarchy is to allow groups to utilize all the rays, if possible, but certainly rays not along their own line. So there is an interrelationship being formed between the various ashrams. When a group soul is formed through Transmission Meditation, you have an entity which can be used by the group to sustain it. You can draw energy from it just as you can draw energy from your own ashramic group.

Transmission is actually taking place on the soul plane. Hierarchy is creating a great network of light throughout the planet. Meditators of all kinds are built into this, but the Transmission groups, in particular, are all connected on the soul plane.

Maitreya, through the process of overshadowing me, is building a network through which He can potentize all the Transmission groups. Eventually, once the second initiation is taken by a large number of people in the groups, He will be able to stimulate directly, along these lines of light, all the people in those Transmission groups. He will not need to act through me then, but will be able to do it directly.

(1) If an area has groups where they are very small in number, would it be an advantage to make an effort to link all together into a larger group when they transmit? (2) Is it important that they transmit at the same time?

Yes, that would be quite a useful thing to do, it only takes a moment in time. They mentally link up for a few moments and that is it, it is done. (2) It does not make much difference because there is no time on that level.

185

Is there a minimum number of people needed for a Transmission group to form a group soul?

Three is a group in Transmission terms. In soul terms, seven would begin to blossom as a soul. Seven people would certainly be able, by the intensity of their interaction, to form a group soul. Their ray structure would be the synthesis of the various members of the group, not just an addition of them, but a synthesis. The group soul will evolve out of the intensity of their work. The work has to be intense; otherwise it does not happen.

Do you know if a Transmission is going to be long?

One of the first rules of discipleship is to forget time. This is absolutely essential. You should throw away your watch. Normally, I never look at my watch during Transmission. You simply go on until it finishes by itself. Either you are working with Hierarchy or you are not working with Hierarchy. People have to realize that these Men — the Masters — are serious. We are not really serious. I find that many people who love to call themselves disciples are rather light-minded in that if they are doing an hour's Transmission they think it is a tremendous thing. They say: "We are a Transmission group, we transmit for an hour then we have tea and cakes and chat." That is not serious.

If you are going to do Transmission Meditation properly, you should be prepared to go for as long as the energies flow, which might be for one hour but probably closer to three, or even four or five hours. You have to be prepared to co-operate with Hierarchy, and not just fit it into your busy life or lazy life or personal life. You have to fit your lazy personal life into the requirement of Hierarchy if you are going to be a disciple. Being a disciple means being disciplined.

Create a rhythm of work and sustain the rhythm. Then you really work in a disciplined way. In terms of time, it is not like saying: "Every day I am going to do this." Then you look at your watch: "Oh, I haven't done it yet", or "Now I've done it."

That is not discipline. Discipline is being prepared to be at the right place at the right time. That is service too. Discipline and service are pretty much the same.

Why was such a promise of taking the second initiation given to us? Won't it have an adverse effect, creating an elitist feeling or arrogance among some people?

Certainly there is that danger, but I assume we are dealing with people with a certain sense of proportion, a certain objectivity, otherwise they would not be involved in service.

The reason this information was given was to enlighten the groups, to lift their hope and aspiration, and to focus their work. The purpose was to give a closer insight into the work of Hierarchy, Their long-term plans, the way in which They work, and to encourage those who may find themselves around 1.5. To know that in this incarnation they are likely to come before the Christ and take the second initiation is an enormously galvanizing idea. Not everybody — some people are not going to do anything with it at all — but most people, knowing that, who are interested in Transmission Meditation, should find that galvanizing, illuminating, and encouraging. That was the purpose: to inform, to encourage, and to stimulate.

What about people who spend perhaps only an hour a week on Transmission? Is mental polarization and the second initiation possible for them too?

I am addressing myself to those who are doing Transmission seriously and are around 1.5 already. An hour a week is not a very intense rhythm; more than that is necessary, I believe.

Why are there not more second or third degree initiates involved in Transmission groups?

Inevitably, since there is no glamour involved (although I am sure people can make glamour out of anything), it draws to it only those who have taken at least the first and perhaps the second initiation. That is not to say that there is no glamour in the groups involved in Transmission Meditation. There is a great deal of glamour in all the groups involved. But the fact that people are in Transmission groups means that on the whole they are not seeking the normal glamours of the average New Age or occult group. They are people who are quite genuinely into service, otherwise they would not do it. But the motive may be mixed. There will almost certainly be a degree of spiritual ambition in the individuals. If they look at themselves, they will find that, at least in part, their motive is self-advancement. But if I made complete freedom from any aspect of glamour a requirement of taking part in a Transmission group, there would be no Transmission groups in the world.

Why are there not more second- or third-degree initiates in Transmission groups? People who have reached the second or third initiation will probably be doing work which would not necessarily involve Transmission Meditation. Nevertheless, whether they are in a formal Transmission group or not, anybody at that level will be transmitting energy in a very potent and purposeful way, because that is the nature of reality; we live in an energetic universe. But that second- or third-degree initiate might be working in the political or economic field or the scientific or educational field. This more esoteric work of Transmission is only one of many fields of activity.

Mao Tse Tung and Winston Churchill were third degree initiates, had never heard of Transmission Meditation, did not know what it was, and probably would not have been interested. Nevertheless, they were transmitters of their particular soul energy. In the case of Winston Churchill, his 2nd-ray soul was behind his actions. With Mao Tse Tung his 1st-ray soul was behind his. (His ray structure was 1-1-1-2-1.) I am sure if you had asked Mao Tse Tung or Winston Churchill if they were third-degree initiates, they would say: "What's that?" They were not the slightest bit interested in the esoteric.

Does a group with people at slightly different points in evolution take initiation at the same time — the slightly more advanced ones having to wait for the slower ones to catch up so that they all go in through the door of initiation together on the same day?

That door, of course, is symbolic. The threshold to initiation is a state of being. It is not actually a door you stand outside waiting for your friends to come up and say: "Hello, I see you got here", and so on. There is no time outside the physical body, and the initiations take place out of the physical body. In this coming time they will also take place on the physical plane, and then it may be you will find your colleagues standing at the door before you.

People go through it as and when they are ready. This depends on their readiness, in occult terms, for initiation. It occurs when the Christ and above all, Sanat Kumara, the Lord of the World, have ascertained that they are absolutely ready for the initiation. The Lord of the World has to be consulted and if He says: "No, not yet", they go back. There is no trial and error in this. You have to be ready; otherwise you would be dead. They are experts. They know whether your chakras will stand the impact of the energy of the Rod directed by the Christ through His own chakras and then through those of two Masters. The initiate stands in the centre of that triangle, and the energy is circulated and then focused by Them through the initiate, where it builds up a great fire resulting in a tremendous heightening of his vibration. But, at the same time, he has already reached that point, which made it possible in the first place. However, it takes him beyond that. So the answer to the questions is, no.

When you are ready and when the astrological influences are right, you can take initiation. If you are ready and they are not, then you cannot; you have to wait until the astrological influences are correct before you can take it. You might be ready and someone else may not be, but then when they are ready, they might be lucky enough to have their astrological influences

189

just right and they might take it before you, who were ready before them. It is very complex. It is group initiation, even today, although you take it individually. Groups are initiated even though they do not know each other. They only see it as an individual thing, but from the point of view of the Hierarchy, it is a group initiation.

The difference in the coming time is that groups will actually take it also on the physical plane. The Christ will go from country to country initiating, in group formation, groups who have prepared themselves in various forms of work — Transmission Meditation is not the only form — for this great achievement.

Although there are many Transmission groups, are we not all together a Transmission Group as a whole?

Yes, that is true. Those who work with me, and they are many people in many countries, form, from the Master's point of view, one group, because they are engaged in the same activity and are availing themselves of this particular Hierarchical attempt or experiment. My Master has made Himself responsible for carrying it out. Through me, He is stimulating groups all over the world — and of course Maitreya even more so — who, together, form an inner group which can work directly and closely with Maitreya in this coming time. This group, wherever they are, form a vanguard for Maitreya: by preparing the way for Him; by doing His work in the world; and being exponents of His energy through whom He can change the World. "I am with you and in you. I seek to express that which I am through you. For this I come."

THE GREAT INVOCATION

From the point of Light within the Mind of God
Let light stream forth into the minds of men.
Let Light descend on Earth.

From the point of Love within the Heart of God
Let love stream forth into the hearts of men.
May Christ return to Earth.

From the centre where the Will of God is known
Let purpose guide the little wills of men —
The Purpose which the Masters know and serve.

From the centre which we call the race of men
Let the Plan of Love and Light work out
And may it seal the door where evil dwells.

Let Light and Love and Power
Restore the Plan on Earth.

FURTHER READING

Books by Benjamin Creme

The Reappearance of the Christ and the Masters of Wisdom
Creme's first book gives the background and pertinent information concerning the return of Maitreya, the Christ, including: the effect of the reappearance on the world's existing institutions, the anti-christ and forces of evil, the soul and reincarnation, meditation, telepathy, nuclear energy, UFOs and ancient civilizations, the problems of the developing world and a new economic order.
ISBN #0-936604-00-X, 256 pp

Maitreya's Mission — Vol. I
Offers much new information on the story of Maitreya's emergence and on such subjects as: the work and teachings of Maitreya, the externalization of the Masters of Wisdom, life ahead in the new age, evolution and initiation, meditation and service, healing and social transformation, the Seven Rays.
3rd Edition. ISBN #90-71484-08-4, 411 pp

Maitreya's Mission — Vol. II
A unique compilation on such subjects as meditation, growth of consciousness, political and economic change, psychology, health, the environment, initiation, group work, world service, and science and technology in the new age. Includes interviews with a Master of Wisdom, as well as the current teachings and forecasts of Maitreya, the World Teacher. Offers provocative explanations for such phenomena as crop circles, crosses of light, visions of the Madonna, healing waters and UFOs.
ISBN #90-71484-11-4, 718 pp

Maitreya's Mission — Vol. III
A chronicle of the next millennium. Political, economic and social structures that will guarantee the necessities of life for all people. New ways of thinking that will reveal the mysteries of the universe and release our divine potential—all guided and inspired by Maitreya and

the Masters of Wisdom. Includes a compilation of the ray structures and points of evolution of 950 initiates throughout history.
ISBN #90-71484-15-7, 704 pp

A Master Speaks
Articles by Benjamin Creme's Master from the first 12 volumes of *Share International* magazine. The book includes such topics as: reason and intuition, health and healing, life in the new age, glamour, human rights, Maitreya's mission, the role of man.
2nd Edition. ISBN #90-71484-10-6, 256 pp

Messages from Maitreya the Christ
During the early years of preparation for His emergence, Maitreya gave 140 messages through Benjamin Creme during public lectures. The method used was mental overshadowing and the telepathic rapport thus set up. The messages inspire readers to spread the news of His reappearance and to work urgently for the rescue of millions suffering from poverty and starvation in a world of plenty.
2nd Edition. ISBN #90-71484-22-X, 286 pp

The Ageless Wisdom Teaching
This introduction to humanity's spiritual legacy covers the major principles: the Divine Plan, source of the teaching, evolution of human consciousness, the Spiritual Hierarchy, energies, the Seven Rays, karma, reincarnation, initiation, and more. Includes a glossary of esoteric terms.
ISBN #90-71484-13-0, 62 pp

֍

The above books have been translated and published in numerous languages. They are available from local bookstores and from various online vendors.

֍

Extensive information on this subject may also be found at:
www.ShareIntl.org
www.TransmissionMeditation.org

Share International

A UNIQUE MAGAZINE featuring each month: • up-to-date information about Maitreya, the World Teacher • an article from a Master of Wisdom • expansions of the esoteric teachings • articles by and interviews with people on the leading edge in every field of endeavor, including: the eradication of hunger and poverty; social and economic change; politics, peace and human rights; science and medicine; psychology and education • news from UN agencies and positive developments in the transformation of our world • Benjamin Creme's answers to a variety of topical questions submitted by subscribers and the public.

Share International brings together the two major directions of new age thinking — the political and the spiritual. It shows the synthesis underlying the political, social, economic and spiritual changes now occurring on a global scale, and seeks to stimulate practical action to rebuild our world along more just and compassionate lines.

Share International covers news, events and comments bearing on Maitreya's priorities: an adequate supply of the right food, adequate housing and shelter for all, healthcare and education as universal rights, the maintenance of ecological balance in the world.

Versions of *Share International* are available in Dutch, French, German, Japanese, Romanian and Spanish. For subscription information, contact the appropriate office below. [ISSN #0169-1341]

For North, Central and South America,
Australia, New Zealand and the Philippines
Share International
P.O. Box 971, North Hollywood, CA 91603 USA

For the UK
Share International
P.O. Box 3677, London NW5 1RU UK

For the rest of the world
Share International
P.O. Box 41877, 1009 DB Amsterdam, Holland

INDEX

A

Ajna centre
  holding attention on
    activates antahkarana,
      141, 151
    creates alignment, 140,
      142
    develops mental
      polarization, 67–69
    learning to work from, 150
    relationship to third eye, 68
Alignment
  definition of, 38
  essential to Transmission,
    136–37
  hindered by mental activity,
    62, 145, 147
  indicated by direction of
    eyes, 147
  recognition of
    requires attention, 140,
      142, 143
    requires awareness of
      etheric energy, 144–45
    varies with bodily
      sensitivities, 141–43
  requires mental focus, 135,
    137

Antahkarana
  brings thought-forms from
    higher mind, 97
  channel for flow of soul
    energy, 60
  created by "holding the
    mind steady in the light",
    95–97
  created by aspiration,
    meditation, service, 71
  role in Transmission, 140
Aquarius, Age of
  astronomical definition of,
    18
  characterized by energy of
    synthesis, 162
  role of humanity in, 90
  will manifest quality of
    Love, 12
Aryan race, 138
Astral planes
  as states of awareness, 39,
    113
  importance of controlling,
    63, 97, 105, 121
  mastered at second
    initiation, 172
  mediumship, 117–19

ABOUT THE AUTHOR

SCOTTISH-BORN PAINTER and esotericist Benjamin Creme has spent the last 26 years preparing the world for the most extraordinary event in humanity's history — the return of our spiritual mentors to the everyday world.

He has appeared on television, radio and in documentary films world-wide, and lectures throughout Western and Eastern Europe, the USA, Japan, Australia, New Zealand, Canada and Mexico.

Trained and supervised over many years by his own Master, he began his public work in 1974. He announced in 1982 that the long-awaited World Teacher, the Lord Maitreya, was residing in London and was ready to present Himself openly when invited to do so by the media. That event is now imminent.

Benjamin Creme continues to perform his task as messenger of this hopeful news. His eight books (soon to be nine) have been translated into many languages. He is also the editor of *Share International* magazine, which circulates in over 70 countries. He accepts no money for any of this work. Benjamin Creme lives in London, is married and has three children.